8-STEP MODEL DRAWING

8-STEP MODEL DRAWING

SINGAPORE'S BEST PROBLEM-SOLVING MATH STRATEGIES

BY BOB HOGAN & CHAR FORSTEN

Crystal Springs
BOOKS
A division of SDE Staff Development for EDUCATORS.

Peterborough, New Hampshire

Published by Crystal Springs Books
A division of Staff Development for Educators (SDE)
10 Sharon Road, PO Box 500
Peterborough, NH 03458
1-800-321-0401
www.crystalsprings.com
www.sde.com

Published 2007
Printed in the United States of America
11 10 09 08   2 3 4 5

ISBN: 978-1-884548-95-6

            Library of Congress Cataloging-in-Publication Data

Hogan, Robert J.
  8-step model drawing : Singapore's best problem-solving math strategies / by Bob Hogan and
Char Forsten.
      p. cm.
  Includes index.
  ISBN 978-1-884548-95-6
  1. Problem solving--Graphic methods. 2. Mathematics--Study and teaching (Elementary) I.
Forsten, Char, 1948- II. Title. III. Title: Eight-step model drawing.

  QA63.H645 2007
  510--dc22

                          2006034110

Editor: Sharon Smith
Art Director, Designer, and Production Coordinator: Soosen Dunholter
Illustrator: Soosen Dunholter

With thanks to my friend, colleague, and mentor, Jim Grant, who handed me a math textbook from Singapore seven years ago and started me on my amazing journey toward helping students better understand math.
—C.F.

To all the students in my math classes at Ashby Elementary School, who made this all possible. I'll forever remember the experience. To my mother, who paved the road with opportunity, guidance, and love. And to my grandparents, whose wisdom helped me become the man I am today.
—B.H.

CONTENTS

ACKNOWLEDGMENTS

We would like to acknowledge and thank:

Richard Bisk, Anne Marie Condike, and Susan Little—all amazing partners in the initial venture of bringing Singapore Math to American classrooms.

Lorraine Walker, Vice President of Staff Development for Educators, who believes passionately in the effectiveness of Singapore Math methods and who has translated her vision into books, manipulatives, and teacher training by us and others.

Sharon Smith, whose role has extended beyond that of editor. Her vision and guidance have made this book what it is—an invaluable resource that will help teachers and students improve their understanding and increase their love of mathematics.

Jana Hazekamp, whose keen eye and years of classroom experience—not to mention her unfailing good humor—were invaluable as she reviewed the manuscript.

Soosen Dunholter, whose artistic design brings life, clarity, and cohesiveness to this book.

Jeffery and Dawn Thomas of SingaporeMath.com, whose friendship and support help us continue our mission to help educators understand and use Singapore's highly effective strategies for teaching math.

Singapore educators, whose methods, especially the model-drawing approach, help us guide students to literally draw conclusions.

AN INTRODUCTION TO MODEL DRAWING

Welcome to the world of model drawing, a powerful problem-solving tool that opens new pathways to learning mathematics for students at every skill level. Whenever we explain this approach to our fellow teachers, we hear choruses of "Awesome!" "Fantastic!" "I wish I'd known about this when *I* was in elementary school!" We feel the same way. Model drawing offers a new way to reach students, using visual models and logical thinking to build problem-solving skills.

Model drawing is just what the name implies: drawing simple visual models to represent word problems. The drawings help students to see—literally—what word problems are all about. This is pretty amazing stuff. And it really works!

How do we know? The model-drawing strategies that we use are adapted from strategies developed in the tiny island nation of Singapore. And why should you care about how math is taught in a country with a population of just 4.5 million? Because, three times in a row, that tiny Asian nation has dramatically outperformed the United States—and every other one of the 45 participating countries—on highly respected international tests.

The tests in question are known as the TIMSS, or the Trends in International Mathematics and Science Study (formerly the Third International Mathematics and Science Study). The TIMSS has been given three times—in 1995, 1999, and 2003. In the most recent study, out of 800 total possible points, Singapore eighth graders topped the charts with an average score of 605.

American students averaged 504, putting the United States in fifteenth place.

Maybe the United States can learn something from Singapore. In the 1980s, we were the ones who were at the top in math and science. Singapore set out to change that—and they succeeded. The way they did it is, we feel, worth emulating in many respects.

In Singapore, math is now taught in the primary grades (one through six) in a specific sequence. Instruction begins at the concrete level, with students using manipulatives to build understanding and mastery of basic concepts and skills. Once they have mastered the fundamentals at the concrete level, students move to the pictorial stage. That pictorial stage is model drawing. Only when students have mastered and internalized the model-drawing process are they ready to advance to more formulaic or algorithmic procedures. This is the final stage of development, known as the abstract stage.

In the United States, as in Singapore, instruction in primary grades generally begins at the concrete stage with the use of manipulatives. The difference is that American instruction usually moves straight from the concrete to the abstract, procedural method of computation. In the intermediate grades and above, instruction typically involves just procedural or abstract math.

The Singapore approach offers a way to bridge the gap between the concrete and abstract levels, reinforcing students' visualization and understanding of math concepts and processes through model drawing. With this approach, when students move on to the abstract level, they have a solid foundation on which to build. They've developed problem-solving skills and real number sense, and they're ready for those abstract concepts.

If we want our students to have the same deep level of understanding that underlies student accomplishment in Singapore, one way to cultivate that understanding is through model drawing. Model drawing is not the *only* aspect of Singapore Math worth emulating in American classrooms—the Singapore approaches to teaching place value and mental math are among the other strategies that are especially strong—but it's an excellent place to start. The beauty of this approach is that it can be used to solve *most* word problems, no matter what the source. We took ten standard American textbook series and applied model drawing to the problems they included. It didn't work in every single case—you still need to teach the other problem-solving strategies, such as Make an Organized List or Work Backward, that are covered in traditional American texts. But we found that model drawing could be used effectively to solve roughly 80 percent of the problems in the texts we tried. And in our experience, the impact on student understanding has been phenomenal.

Clearly, we and other teachers who have used model drawing think this is an incredibly effective way to teach math. But you need to see for yourself, and that's why we've created this book.

What This Book Is & Is Not

This book is an introduction to model drawing. It includes illustrated practice problems to help teachers and students learn this highly effective approach to solving word problems. It shows how to apply this approach to word problems involving numerous basic math operations and functions taught in grades one through six. It is intended to help educators in schools currently using or adopting the whole Singapore Math program, as well as those who choose to supplement their American texts by using the model-drawing approach to solve word problems from their current texts.

This book is *not* a resource for teaching all of the commonly used heuristics—Guess and Check, Use or Make an Organized List, Look for Patterns, Work Backward, Use Logic, Draw a Picture or a Diagram, and so on—for solving word problems. These are all important and effective strategies for students to learn and use, and they are critical components of math programs currently in use in the United States. Because these heuristics are already covered so thoroughly elsewhere, we chose to focus this book solely on the model-drawing approach.

> **The way to learn model drawing is to begin *using* model drawing—but, like anything else, it helps to begin with guided practice.**

How to Use This Book

The way to learn model drawing is to begin *using* model drawing—but, like anything else, it helps to begin with guided practice. So that's exactly what we've provided: plenty of guided practice. With each of the first 20 problems included here, we walk you through the model-drawing process one simple, straightforward step at a time. With every problem, we review the specific steps, model the process, and offer suggested language you can use to guide your students through the individual problems.

The modeling for each example is based on Bob Hogan's process of 8-Step Model Drawing. We recommend that you start by reading through the list of the steps in the process (page 18). This list may not mean much to you until you've walked through some sample problems, but since these steps are the key to the process, it's worth looking them over before going any further.

That done, you'll probably want to begin at the very beginning of the guided practice problems—no matter what level you teach. The concepts of model drawing are introduced incrementally here because that's how you'd introduce them to your students. We've found that even if you're teaching intermediate students, it helps to start by demonstrating how the process works with basic addition. By doing this, you help students separate process from content. They learn how to apply the model-drawing process to a variety of operations, without being asked to perform challenging computations at the same time.

With each guided practice lesson, you'll find one or more key points (labeled "Hold These Thoughts") to remember as you and your students continue with model drawing. These are the building blocks that help establish proficiency.

With practice, students master the process and are able to use it with increasingly more complex math problems. At that point, and only at that point, you may want to turn to the condensed version of the 8 Steps of Model Drawing (page 19) and begin using that as a common reference point. (For space reasons, it's that condensed version that we've repeated throughout each of the guided practice problems in this book.)

As you work with your students on the eight basic steps, you'll want to keep in mind two more lessons from Singapore: focus on one thing at a time, and go for mastery. You may well be used to covering 5 to 10 word problems a day. In Singapore, students spend 10 to 15 minutes every day focusing on just one word problem. There are two critical elements here: "every day" and "focus." Your students need to work with model drawing *every single day,* and they need to do it intensively.

Here again we can learn from Singapore, where teachers use a method of intensive questioning that engages students and allows them to feel success immediately ("Who can read this word problem?" "Who are we talking about in this problem?"). Teachers then build on that success to help students discover new concepts and skills ("Which is greater, 3 or 4? How can we show that in this drawing? . . . Now, what's the ratio of Ty's books to Ling's?").

▭▶ **The concepts of model drawing are introduced incrementally here because that's how you'd introduce them to your students.**

Good teachers are good questioners. That's nothing new, but it's critical to building mastery of model drawing. That's why we've provided specific language to demonstrate how you might present model drawing to your students through the questioning process.

Along with each of these sample lessons, we've also included a section called "Milking the Problem for All It's Worth." Here you'll find examples of other questions you can use to generate further learning based on the information provided in the problem. This is one of the many advantages of model drawing: unlike most American approaches, which typically answer only the question asked, model drawing literally illustrates the answers to all kinds of questions that could be asked about that same information. Once again, you're creating new pathways to learning.

One Answer, Many Paths

It's at this point that model drawing connects to differentiated instruction. Differentiated instruction, as you know, is all about reaching different students through different pathways, whether that means differentiating by interest, skill level, learning style, or multiple intelligences. Model drawing gives you a way to address all of those differences in your classroom.

You can use the drawings to encourage new understandings at whatever level is appropriate for each student and in whatever way will best capture that student's interest. You can also use the drawings to demonstrate that many types of computation will result in the same answer. "Who can solve this problem? Right! How did you get that answer? You added 24 + 24 + 24 to get 72? Great! Anybody else have another way? You used mental math? How? You multiplied 25 times 3 and then subtracted 3 to get 72? Terrific! Anybody else?" All students can experience success—and that makes them excited about math and ready to go to the next level.

The computation piece of model drawing is not the only place where students can reach the correct answer in more than one way. Sometimes there are perfectly legitimate alternative ways to handle the drawings themselves. With each of the problems in this book, we've tried to demonstrate the approach that would make the most sense at the grade level when students are likely to first encounter the problem. For example, the problem that begins on page 23

> **Unlike most American approaches, which typically answer only the question asked, model drawing literally illustrates the answers to all kinds of questions that could be asked about that same information.**

shows a separate unit for each item involved because in first grade, when this kind of single-digit addition problem is generally taught, students need to see the individual units. We show that problem like this:

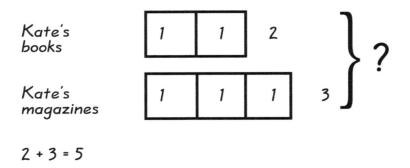

2 + 3 = 5

When presenting this problem in first grade, you might want to give students copies of the graph paper reproducible on page 155 to help with the mechanical aspect of the drawing. To make things more concrete, you might even want to have them substitute Unifix cubes or color tiles for the drawings. But when working with older students, you can go to a different level. You can still use this basic problem to introduce the model-drawing process, but at that grade level it would, of course, be entirely appropriate to illustrate it with just two unit bars, extending the second one proportionately. The result would look something like this:

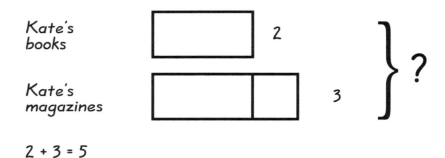

2 + 3 = 5

What's Next?

As you walk your students through the guided practice problems, questioning them every step of the way, you'll also want to give them opportunities for *independent* practice. We've included reproducible problems (pages 94–149) for just that purpose—along with the answers *and* examples of the drawings that can help students to reach those answers.

So when and where do you start? Clearly, the key to making model drawing work for your students is repeated and consistent practice. The more a student practices using model drawing, the more adept he will become at using it. Once he's internalized the process, he can focus on the content.

Having said that, our best advice is simply to start. Now. Try model drawing for yourself, and then with your students. Imagine your students independently solving word problems.

What a picture!

8 STEPS OF MODEL DRAWING

Setting Up the Model

1. Read the entire problem.

2. Determine who is involved in the problem. List vertically in the order each appears in the problem.

3. Determine what is involved in the problem. List beside the "who" from the previous step.

4. Draw unit bars of equal length.

Solving the Problem

5. Reread the problem, one sentence at a time, plugging the information into the visual model. Stop at each comma and illustrate the information on the unit bar.

   If a sentence does not contain commas, but has too much information, chunk or break the sentence into smaller parts.

6. Determine the question and place the question mark in the appropriate place in the drawing.

7. Work all computation to the right side or underneath the drawing.

8. Answer the question in a complete sentence, or as a longer response if asked.

8 STEPS OF MODEL DRAWING

1. **Read** the entire problem.

2. Decide **who** is involved in the problem.

3. Decide **what** is involved in the problem.

4. **Draw** unit bars of equal length.

5. **Read** each sentence, one at a time.

6. Put the **question mark** in place.

7. **Work computation** to the side or underneath.

8. **Answer** the question in a complete sentence.

PROBLEMS
FOR GUIDED
PRACTICE

ADDITION

Kate read 2 books. She also read 3 magazines. How many books and magazines did she read altogether?

....

STEP ONE: *Read the entire problem.*

> Kate read 2 books. She also read 3 magazines. How many books and magazines did she read altogether?

STEP TWO: *Decide who is involved in the problem.*

Kate

STEP THREE: *Decide what is involved in the problem.*

Kate's
books

Kate's
magazines

STEP FOUR: *Draw unit bars of equal length.*

Kate's
books

Kate's
magazines

" Teacher Talk "

STEP ONE: *Let's read the entire problem and picture what is going on.*

STEP TWO: *Who is involved in the problem? That's correct: Kate. Is anyone else involved in this problem? No, just Kate. Let's write her name on the left side of our work.*

STEP THREE: *Now that we know Kate is involved in the problem, we can ask, "Kate's what?" What are we talking about? Is it Kate's money, her pets, her buttons? Look at the question and tell me what it is we are talking about. Great! We're talking about Kate's books and Kate's magazines. We have 2 variables, so we need to list each variable separately. First we'll write "books" next to Kate's name, so it reads, "Kate's books." Why did we use an apostrophe? That's correct: to show that the books belong to Kate.*

Now, are we talking about just 1 variable? Are we talking about just Kate's books? No, we're talking about Kate's books and what? That's right: Kate's magazines. So let's write "Kate's magazines" right below "Kate's books."

STEP FOUR: *In this next step, we need to draw 1 unit bar directly to the right of each variable. Who can tell me what a variable is? How many variables do we have? That's right: we have 2. So we need 1 unit bar for "Kate's books" and 1 unit bar for "Kate's magazines." This is what a unit bar looks like. We need to draw 2 of them. And we need to be sure both unit bars are the same size.*

Now that we've set up the problem, we can begin to solve it through model drawing.

STEP FIVE: *Read each sentence, one at a time.*

A

"Kate read 2 books."

Kate's
books

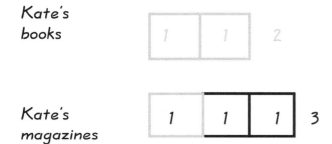

Kate's
magazines

B

"She also read 3 magazines."

Kate's
books

Kate's
magazines

C

"How many books and magazines did she read altogether?"

STEP FIVE—A: *We need to read the story and stop after every sentence to see what we've learned. Let's read the first sentence. "Kate read 2 books." What information does it give us? You're correct: we learn that Kate read 2 books. If the first unit bar represents each book she read, do we have all the units we need? No, we do not. How many unit bars do we need? Let's add 1 more. How big should we make it? That's right: exactly the same size as the first one. Let's draw that unit bar right next to the first one we drew, so there's no space between them. What number should we write inside each of those unit bars for books? And what number should we write at the end to show how many books Kate read? 2? Wonderful!*

B: *Now we can move on to the second sentence, which tells us that Kate also read 3 magazines. How do we show those 3 magazines? That's it: add 2 more unit bars. How big do we make them? The same size as the others. What do we write in each one? And what do we write at the end? 3? Yes!*

C: *Let's read the last sentence: "How many books and magazines did she read altogether?" That brings us to the question.*

HOLD THESE THOUGHTS

☛ Be sure all the unit bars for each variable are touching each other so comparisons are clearer.

☛ At the beginning of first grade, show one unit for each item.

STEP SIX: Put the question mark in place.

STEP SEVEN: Work computation to the side or underneath.

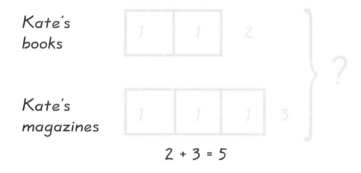

$$2 + 3 = 5$$

STEP EIGHT: Answer the question in a complete sentence.

Kate read 5 books and magazines altogether.

STEP SIX: What's the question? What do we need to find out? Are we looking for how many books and magazines Kate read in all? Yes! Where will we write our question mark in our model? What's the question we need to answer? Very good! Let's write the question mark to the right of the unit bars, using a brace to show that we're looking for the total. This is how we draw a brace.

STEP SEVEN: How are we going to figure out the answer to this question? What numbers do we see in the problem? What should we do? Should we subtract them? No, we should add them, shouldn't we? Now, tell me how we might add these numbers. Sure, one way is to write "2 + 3 = 5." Let's show our work when doing the adding. Who did it another way? Could we also count the individual units? Absolutely! Whichever way we figure it, do we get the same answer? We sure do! Now we need to record our thinking to show how we got the answer.

STEP EIGHT: We need to write a complete sentence to answer the question. Look at the question to get ideas for the answer. Can we borrow some words from the question to get the answer? That's right: "Kate read 5 books and magazines altogether." We always answer the question in a complete sentence.

MILKING THE PROBLEM FOR ALL IT'S WORTH

▐▶   **How many more magazines than books did Kate read ?**

▐▶   **If Kate wanted to read 4 books, how many more would she need to read?**

ADDITION

Alicia had $6 more than Bobby. If Bobby had $10, how much did they have altogether?

....

STEP ONE: *Read the entire problem.*

> "Alicia had $6 more than Bobby. If Bobby had $10, how much did they have altogether?"

STEP TWO: *Decide who is involved in the problem.*

Alicia

Bobby

STEP THREE: *Decide what is involved in the problem.*

Alicia's money

Bobby's money

" Teacher Talk "

STEP ONE: *Let's begin by reading the entire problem.*

STEP TWO: *Who is involved in this problem? We want to list all of the people who are involved. To the left side of the paper, we need to list the people vertically, in the order they appear in the problem. Alicia and Bobby are involved. Great! List the names vertically. What does "vertically" mean? That's right: one below the other.*

STEP THREE: *Now that we know the names of the people, Alicia and Bobby, we can ask, "Alicia's and Bobby's what?" What are we talking about? Is it their books? Their buttons? Their money? We need to list the "what" right next to the "who." This will tell us how many variables we are working with in this problem.*

What are we talking about? "Money" is correct! We want to write "money" next to both Alicia's and Bobby's names. Remember to put an apostrophe and an "s" to show that the money belongs to Alicia and to Bobby.

HOLD THESE THOUGHTS

- ☞ In the drawing, list the variables in the order they appear in the problem.
- ☞ Stress vocabulary. Even in the lower grades, ask how many variables are involved.

STEP FOUR: Draw unit bars of equal length.

Alicia's money

```
┌─────────────┐
│             │
│             │
└─────────────┘
```

Bobby's money

```
┌─────────────┐
│             │
└─────────────┘
```

STEP FIVE: Read each sentence, one at a time.

A

"Alicia had $6 more than Bobby."

Alicia's money

```
┌──────────┬──────┐
│          │  $6  │
└──────────┴──────┘
```

Bobby's money

```
┌──────────┐
│          │
└──────────┘
```

B

"If Bobby had $10, . . ."

Alicia's money

```
┌──────────┬──────┐
│          │  $6  │
└──────────┴──────┘
```

Bobby's money

```
┌──────────┐
│   $10    │
└──────────┘
```

C

". . . how much did they have altogether?"

STEP FOUR: *We have determined that we have 2 variables in this problem. What are the 2 variables? Alicia's money and Bobby's money. So now we need to draw 2 unit bars—1 next to Alicia's name and 1 next to Bobby's.*

Let's review all of the steps thus far. We read the problem in its entirety. Then we determined who was involved in the problem: Alicia and Bobby. Next, we determined that the problem was about their money. We listed "money" next to both Bobby's and Alicia's names. Finally we drew unit bars for both variables. We are ready to go to Step Five.

STEP FIVE—A: *Remember, as we reread we need to stop after each sentence. Begin with the first sentence: "Alicia had $6 more than Bobby." Who had more money? Yes, Alicia. How much more money did Alicia have? Right: $6. Who had less money? How much less money did Bobby have than Alicia? Which bar should be longer? Alicia's! By how much? Does Alicia's bar look longer right now? Should we add on to her bar? By how much? Can we add another bar that's about half as long as the first one? Absolutely!*

Great! We added another unit onto Alicia's bar. This new unit is worth $6, so let's write "$6" in that unit.

B: *Now let's go on to sentence two. "If Bobby had $10, how much did they have altogether?" Wow! There's too much information here! Let's read this sentence again and stop when we find a new piece of information. Where should we stop? At the comma!*

Let's try it again. "If Bobby had $10, . . ." We'll pause here because of the what? Yes, the comma! Who are we talking about now? Are we talking about Alicia? Who are we talking about? Bobby? Yes! Which bar should we be concerned about filling in? Yes, Bobby's. How much money did Bobby have? $10! Where should this amount be placed? Should we put this amount in Alicia's bar? Why not?

C: *Let's continue reading sentence two: ". . . how much did they have altogether?"*

Since we are at the end of the question, we can now go to Step Six.

STEP SIX: Put the question mark in place.

STEP SEVEN: Work computation to the side or underneath.

$$\$10 + \$10 = \$20$$
$$\$20 + \$6 = \$26$$

OR

$$\$10 + \$6 = \$16$$
$$\$16 + \$10 = \$26$$

STEP EIGHT: Answer the question in a complete sentence.

Alicia and Bobby had $26 altogether.

STEP SIX: *Think about what the question is asking. Are we looking for just Bobby's money? Are we looking for just Alicia's money? Are we looking for both Bobby's and Alicia's money? Right! So we can add a question mark. Let's link all of the bars with a brace and then add a question mark.*

STEP SEVEN: *Since all of the bars have not been filled in yet, let's fill in the last bar before we begin computing. Do we know the value of this bar? How can you tell the value of this bar? Great! It is $10 because it matches the bar right below it.*

Now, how are we going to figure out the answer to the question? What should we do? Why? Great! Let's add.

Give me suggestions for adding. Sure! Take 10 and add 10 to equal 20. Then add 6 ones to equal 26. How about another suggestion? Take 10 plus 6, which equals 16? Now add 10 to that? Great! The answer is again 26.

STEP EIGHT: *How should this question be answered? Remember: always write the answer in a complete sentence. "Alicia and Bobby had $26 altogether." Fantastic!*

MILKING THE PROBLEM FOR ALL IT'S WORTH

➠ How much money did Bobby have?

➠ How much money did Alicia have?

➠ What things could you buy for $26?

SUBTRACTION

Mia had 14 baseball cards. She gave 5 away and kept the rest for herself. How many cards did Mia have left for herself?

....

STEP ONE: *Read the entire problem.*

"Mia had 14 baseball cards. She gave 5 away and kept the rest for herself. How many cards did Mia have left for herself?"

STEP TWO: *Decide who is involved in the problem.*

Mia

STEP THREE: *Decide what is involved in the problem.*

Mia's
baseball
cards

STEP FOUR: *Draw unit bars of equal length.*

Mia's
baseball   [unit bar]
cards

STEP FIVE: *Read each sentence, one at a time.*

A

"Mia had 14 baseball cards."

Mia's
baseball   [unit bar]   14
cards

" Teacher Talk "

STEP ONE: *Let's read the entire problem.*

STEP TWO: *Who is involved in this problem? Yes, we're talking about Mia. Is anyone else involved in this problem? No, only Mia. Let's write "Mia" on the left side of our work.*

STEP THREE: *Now that we know who we are talking about, we can ask, "Mia's what?" What are we talking about? Is it Mia's lunch? Her stickers? That's correct: we're talking about her baseball cards. We need to write "baseball cards" right below Mia's name. Why did we use an apostrophe and an "s"? That's correct: to show that the baseball cards belong to Mia.*

STEP FOUR: *In this next step, we need to draw a unit bar directly to the right of the variable. How many variables do we have? So how many unit bars do we need? Great! We have just 1 variable, so we need just 1 unit bar.*

STEP FIVE—A: *Let's read the first sentence. What information does it give us? That's right: We learn that Mia had 14 baseball cards. Is this her total number of baseball cards? Where should we write the total? Yes, let's write the total to the right of the unit bar.*

B

"She gave 5 away . . ."

Mia's
baseball
cards

      5   14
      G

C

". . . and kept the rest for herself."

Mia's
baseball
cards
K   5   14
          G

D

"How many cards did Mia have left for herself?"

B: Now, let's go on to the second sentence. What's the problem with this sentence? Too much information! So let's "chunk" it, or break it into pieces. If we read just the first part, it says, "She gave 5 away." Let's mark off a part of our unit bar, near the end, and let's write a 5 inside that piece. Should we also give that piece a label, so we can remember what it shows? What would be a good label? "G" for "gave away"? Sounds good to me!

Now let's think about what's happening here. What's Mia doing? Is she going to have more cards or fewer cards? That's right: fewer. If we want to show that she's ending up with fewer cards, we're going to have to cross some out. So let's put a slash through the part with the 5 to show that those 5 are gone. Does everyone understand what we're doing? When we're subtracting, we mark off a segment at the end of the unit bar, and we put a slash through it to show that that part's gone away; we got rid of it.

C: Now let's finish the sentence. What does it tell us? She kept the rest for herself. Do we need to change anything in our unit bar to show that? No, we do not. How about adding a label to the other part of the unit bar? What would be a good label to add? "K" for "kept"? Absolutely!

D: We're ready for the last sentence: "How many cards did Mia have left for herself?" That brings us to the question.

HOLD THIS THOUGHT

☛ To show subtraction, mark off the appropriate segment of the unit bar and draw a diagonal slash mark through it.

STEP SIX: *Put the question mark in place.*

Mia's
baseball
cards

STEP SEVEN: *Work computation to the side or underneath.*

Mia's
baseball
cards

$14 - 5 = 9$

STEP EIGHT: *Answer the question in a complete sentence.*

Mia had 9 baseball cards left for herself.

STEP SIX: *Are we looking for the total number of Mia's baseball cards? No, we already know that she had a total of 14. What are we being asked to do in this problem? You're correct: we're asked to figure out how many baseball cards Mia had left for herself after she gave 5 away.*

Who can tell us what we're trying to solve in mathematical language? Great! We're trying to figure out what part of 14 was left after Mia gave 5 cards away. And which part of the unit bar shows what we're trying to figure out? Correct again. Let's put the question mark inside the first part of the unit bar.

STEP SEVEN: *Who recognizes what kind of a problem we have? Yes, it's a "whole-part-part." We are given the total and 1 part, so we need to figure out the other part. What should we do to solve this? That's correct: we're going to subtract. How do you know? Now, who can tell me what we'll subtract? What numbers do we have in this problem?*

Great! Let's write "14 – 5 = 9." How many cards did Mia have left for herself? 9! Correct!

STEP EIGHT: *Now we can finish the problem. How should this question be answered in a complete sentence? Very good. "Mia had 9 baseball cards left for herself."*

MILKING THE PROBLEM FOR ALL IT'S WORTH

➠ **In the end, how many more cards did Mia keep than she gave away?**

➠ **After she gave 5 cards away, how many cards would Mia need if she wanted 30 in her collection?**

SUBTRACTION

Christine has $24 in her piggy bank. If she spends $8 on a gift, how much money will she have left in her piggy bank?

STEP ONE: *Read the entire problem.*

"Christine has $24 in her piggy bank. If she spends $8 on a gift, how much money will she have left in her piggy bank?"

STEP TWO: *Decide who is involved in the problem.*

Christine

STEP THREE: *Decide what is involved in the problem.*

Christine's
money

STEP FOUR: *Draw unit bars of equal length.*

Christine's
money ▢

" Teacher Talk "

STEP ONE: *Let's read the problem.*

STEP TWO: *Who's involved in this problem? What is the name of the person involved in this problem? That's right: Christine. Where should we put the name of this person? Yes, on the left side of our work.*

STEP THREE: *We know that Christine is the person involved in this problem. We need to find out what goes along with Christine. Should we put a label of "Christine's piggy bank" or "Christine's money"? Which should we use? Why?*

Great! We have "Christine's money" as our label. When we look at the actual question line of the problem, it asks us how much she has left. It is the money that we are looking for in this problem.

STEP FOUR: *How many variables do we have in this problem? Just 1? Right! And what's that 1 variable again? Christine's money? Right! Therefore, how many bars must we draw? Fantastic job! We need 1 unit bar.*

STEP FIVE: *Read each sentence, one at a time.*
A

"Christine has $24 in her piggy bank."

Christine's money
[   ] $24

STEP FIVE—A: *Let's read the first sentence. "Christine has $24 in her piggy bank." In the unit bar marked "Christine's money," where could we put the value of $24? Yes, we could put the amount in the bar, but since we have only 1 bar and "24" represents the total, let's put the value at the end of the bar.*

B

"If she spends $8 on a gift, . . ."

Christine's money
[\$8 / G] $24

B: *Let's continue reading. "If she spends $8 on a gift, . . ." Pause for the comma. What's happening to Christine's money? Is she adding to it or subtracting from it? So what do we need to do to the unit bar? Do we need to add to it? No! We need to subtract, or take a piece off from it. Remember how we do that? Right! With subtraction, or an amount that we need to take away, we mark off a segment of the unit bar and label it. In this case, we'll label it "$8." Let's also label this piece "G" for "gift" so we always know what that piece stands for. Next, we'll put a diagonal slash mark through that unit to show the money's gone.*

C

". . . how much money will she have left in her piggy bank?"

C: *Let's read on: ". . . how much money will she have left in her piggy bank?" This brings us to the question.*

STEP SIX: *Put the question mark in place.*

Christine's money
[? L | \$8 / G] $24

STEP SIX: *Since $8 is clearly marked and now discarded, we know that the part of the unit bar that is not filled in must represent the amount that we are looking for in this particular problem. So we'll label this with a question mark as well as an "L" for "left."*

HOLD THIS THOUGHT

☛ Include labels to help clarify drawings.

STEP SEVEN: Work computation to the side or underneath.

Christine's money

$$\$24 - \$8 = \$16$$

OR

$$\$24 - \$10 = \$14$$
$$\$14 + \$2 = \$16$$

STEP EIGHT: Answer the question in a complete sentence.

Christine will have $16 left in her piggy bank after spending $8 on a gift.

STEP SEVEN: *How are we going to go about solving this? How do you know if this is an addition problem or a subtraction problem? Look at the diagram and infer, "what plus $8 equals $24?" You can also start with the whole $24 and subtract out $8. Note the whole-to-part relationships.*

Use counting-back strategies or a traditional algorithm to solve this problem. What is $24 – $8? Correct! What else could you do? Yes, mental math works well. We can take $24 – $10 to get $14 and then add $2 to get $16.

STEP EIGHT: *How would you answer the question in a complete sentence? "Christine will have $16 left in her piggy bank after spending $8 on a gift."*

MILKING THE PROBLEM FOR ALL IT'S WORTH

▶ What items might you buy that cost $8?

▶ How much money would Christine have to put in her piggy bank to double the original money in the piggy bank?

MULTIPLICATION

Lu has 3 plates of cupcakes. There are 4 cupcakes on each plate. How many cupcakes does Lu have altogether?

STEP ONE: *Read the entire problem.*

"Lu has 3 plates of cupcakes. There are 4 cupcakes on each plate. How many cupcakes does Lu have altogether?"

STEP TWO: *Decide who is involved in the problem.*

Lu

STEP THREE: *Decide what is involved in the problem.*

Lu's
cupcakes

STEP FOUR: *Draw unit bars of equal length.*

Lu's
cupcakes

STEP ONE: *Let's read the entire problem.*

STEP TWO: *Who is involved in this problem? That's right: we're talking about Lu. We need to write her name below the problem on the left.*

STEP THREE: *Now that we know we're talking about Lu, we need to decide what it is we're talking about. Lu's what? Is it her stamps? Her books? Her cupcakes! How do you know? Okay, let's add "cupcakes" below "Lu." Notice we need to use an apostrophe and an "s." What does this mean again? Great! It means that the cupcakes belong to Lu.*

STEP FOUR: *How many variables do we have? That's right: since we've determined that we're talking about Lu's cupcakes, we have just 1 variable. We need to draw just 1 unit bar, to the right.*

STEP FIVE: *Read each sentence, one at a time.*

A

"Lu has 3 plates of cupcakes."

Lu's
cupcakes

plate   plate   plate

B

"There are 4 cupcakes on each plate."

Lu's
cupcakes

4	4	4

plate   plate   plate

C

"How many cupcakes does Lu have altogether?"

STEP SIX: *Put the question mark in place.*

Lu's
cupcakes

4	4	4	?

plate   plate   plate

STEP FIVE—A: *Let's read the first sentence. "Lu has 3 plates of cupcakes." How many plates? Yes, 3. Let's look at the unit bar. Right now we have just 1 unit bar. What could we do to show 3 equal groups? Great! We can add 2 more unit bars to show 3 equal parts. Let's write "plate" under each unit bar to remind us what we're talking about. We've now illustrated the information in the first sentence.*

B: *Let's go on to the second sentence. "There are 4 cupcakes on each plate." How many cupcakes are on each plate? 4! Think about this. We now have 3 equal unit bars that stand for Lu's plates. How many cupcakes do we need to show on each plate? Let's write "4" in each of the 3 unit bars. Now our model shows Lu's 3 plates with 4 cupcakes on each plate.*

C: *Let's read the last sentence. "How many cupcakes does Lu have altogether?" What does that brings us to? The question!*

STEP SIX: *What is the question we're asked to solve? If we want to know how many cupcakes Lu has altogether, where should we write our question mark? Great! We'll put it to the right of the unit bar to show that we need to find her total number of cupcakes.*

HOLD THIS THOUGHT

☞ Typically, when multiplying, you draw additional units onto the end of the initial unit bar.

STEP SEVEN: *Work computation to the side or underneath.*

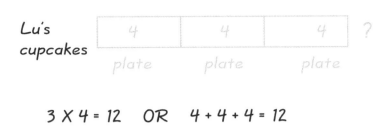

Lu's cupcakes

$$3 \times 4 = 12 \quad OR \quad 4 + 4 + 4 = 12$$

STEP EIGHT: *Answer the question in a complete sentence.*

Lu has 12 cupcakes altogether.

STEP SEVEN: *How are we going to figure out the answer to this question? Should we add, subtract, or multiply? Why? You're right! We can either add or multiply. Now, what numbers do we have in our drawing? If we have 3 groups of 4, and we want to use multiplication, how would we do that? Yes! We'd say 3 X 4 = 12. Let's show that below the problem. And if we wanted to* add *the numbers, how would we do that? That's right. We'd say 4 + 4 + 4 = 12. Either way, we get 12.*

STEP EIGHT: *How should this question be answered? Echo the question in the answer. Absolutely! "Lu has 12 cupcakes altogether."*

MILKING THE PROBLEM FOR ALL IT'S WORTH

➠ How many more cupcakes would Lu need if she wanted a total of 18 cupcakes?

➠ If she had 18 cupcakes and she wanted 3 cupcakes on each plate, how many plates would she need?

➠ What if she had only 2 plates with 3 cupcakes on each plate? How many total cupcakes would she have then?

MULTIPLICATION

At lunch recess Karen passed out 3 times as many cookies as Vito did. If Vito passed out 35 cookies, how many cookies did they pass out altogether?

STEP ONE: *Read the entire problem.*

"At lunch recess Karen passed out 3 times as many cookies as Vito did. If Vito passed out 35 cookies, how many cookies did they pass out altogether?"

STEP TWO: *Decide who is involved in the problem.*

Karen

Vito

STEP THREE: *Decide what is involved in the problem.*

Karen's
cookies

Vito's
cookies

STEP FOUR: *Draw unit bars of equal length.*

Karen's
cookies

Vito's
cookies

" Teacher Talk "

STEP ONE: *Let's read the problem.*

STEP TWO: *Who is involved in this problem? Who are these people? Yes, Karen. Yes, Vito. Is there anyone else? No. Who should appear first when writing down the names? That's right: in our drawing, we want to list the names in the order they appear in the problem, so we'll list Karen first.*

STEP THREE: *We have Karen and Vito. We are talking about their what? Where should we list "cookies"? Great. Let's put "cookies" under both "Karen" and "Vito," so we can see that we're talking about Karen's cookies and Vito's cookies. What do we call Karen's and Vito's cookies in terms of mathematics? Yes! We call them variables.*

STEP FOUR: *Since we have 2 variables, we need to have 2 unit bars. Remember that we need to make both unit bars the same length when beginning a problem. If we need to, we can manipulate the size of the bars during Step Five.*

HOLD THIS THOUGHT

☞ Initially, draw one unit bar for each variable.

STEP FIVE: *Read each sentence, one at a time.*

A

"At lunch recess Karen passed out 3 times as many cookies as Vito did."

Karen's cookies

Vito's cookies

B

"If Vito passed out 35 cookies, . . ."

Karen's cookies

Vito's cookies | 35

C

". . . how many cookies did they pass out altogether?"

STEP FIVE—A: *One by one, read each sentence. Let's start with the first sentence. "At lunch recess Karen passed out 3 times as many cookies as Vito did." We need to look at which person we're talking about in this sentence. Who are we talking about? Karen? Yes! Right now does our picture look like Karen passed out 3 times as many cookies as Vito? Or does it look like she passed out the same number of cookies? If I draw another equally sized unit bar next to Karen's bar, is that depicting 3 times as many as Vito? Why or why not? How many more bars do I need to draw next to Karen's original bar? Why don't I draw 3 more unit bars? Right: that would give us 4 in all, and that would be too many.*

So I'll draw 2 more bars, giving us 3 bars in all for Karen. This represents 3 times as many.

B: *Let's go on to the next sentence. "If Vito passed out 35 cookies, how many cookies did they pass out altogether?" What's wrong with this sentence? Too much information! So where do we stop? That's right: at the comma.*

Let's try it again. "If Vito passed out 35 cookies, . . ." What do I do here? That's right: pause because of the comma. Before we continue with the sentence, let's work with the drawing to show what we have so far in the sentence.

If Vito has 35 cookies, I can label his bar with the number 35. Should I label anything for Karen? No, no, no! The sentence doesn't mention anything about Karen, so I shouldn't write any numbers in Karen's unit bars.

C: *What's the final part of the sentence? ". . . how many cookies did they pass out altogether?" That brings us to the question that is being asked in this particular problem.*

HOLD THIS THOUGHT

☛ When a problem says, "There were three times as many, . . ." add one unit bar at a time. Otherwise, many students will add *three* more unit bars instead of adding just two.

STEP SIX: *Put the question mark in place.*

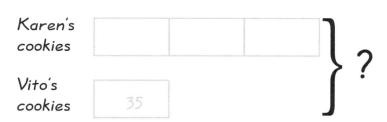

Karen's cookies

Vito's cookies

35

}

?

STEP SIX: *Since we want to know what all of the bars together are worth, we'll add a brace to the right of the unit bars to connect them, and we'll add a question mark to the right of the brace. That shows "altogether." We want to know the value of all 4 bars combined.*

STEP SEVEN: *Work computation to the side or underneath.*

Karen's cookies

| 35 | 35 | 35 |

Vito's cookies

35

}

?

4 X 35 = 140

OR

35 + 35 = 70
70 X 2 = 140

OR

30 X 4 = 120
5 X 4 = 20
120 + 20 = 140

OR

35 + 35 + 35 + 35 = 140

STEP SEVEN: *Before we can compute, we know that each bar is worth what amount? 35? How do we know that? If Vito's unit bar is worth 35 and all the unit bars are the same size, is every one of them worth 35? Absolutely! Let's put "35" in each of the unlabeled bars.*

Now, how would you compute the answer? What do you see in our drawing? Great! 4 X 35 = 140. Anybody else? Yes, we could say 35 + 35 = 70 and then double that to get 140. Anybody else? Yes, we could use the distributive property. We could multiply 30 X 4 to get 120 and 5 X 4 to get 20, and then add 120 + 20 to get 140. Any other ideas? Sure, we could add 35 + 35 + 35 + 35 and get 140. Those are all ways to get the answer: 140.

HOLD THIS THOUGHT

☞ The computation is the differentiated part of the lesson. The model looks the same for all students, but the way they achieve success with computation is differentiated.

STEP EIGHT: *Answer the question in a complete sentence.*

Karen and Vito passed out 140 cookies altogether during lunch recess.

STEP EIGHT: *How would you answer the question? "Karen and Vito passed out 140 cookies altogether during lunch recess."*

MILKING THE PROBLEM FOR ALL IT'S WORTH

▶ How many cookies did Karen pass out at recess?

▶ What is the ratio of Karen's cookies to Vito's cookies?

▶ What fraction of all the cookies passed out were given by Karen?

DIVISION

Carlos has 8 marbles in his backpack. If he takes them out and divides them into 4 equal groups, how many marbles will be in each group?

....

STEP ONE: *Read the entire problem.*

> "Carlos has 8 marbles in his backpack. If he takes them out and divides them into 4 equal groups, how many marbles will be in each group?"

STEP TWO: *Decide who is involved in the problem.*

Carlos

STEP THREE: *Decide what is involved in the problem.*

Carlos's marbles

STEP FOUR: *Draw unit bars of equal length.*

Carlos's marbles

STEP FIVE: *Read each sentence, one at a time.*

A

"Carlos has 8 marbles in his backpack."

Carlos's marbles   8

" Teacher Talk "

STEP ONE: *Let's read the entire problem.*

STEP TWO: *Who is involved in this problem? That's right: it's Carlos. Let's write his name on the left, below the problem.*

STEP THREE: *What are we talking about in this problem? Carlos's what? Great! We're talking about Carlos's marbles. Let's write "marbles" below "Carlos" so we have "Carlos's marbles." Remind me what the apostrophe means? Yes, it means the marbles belong to Carlos.*

STEP FOUR: *How many variables do we have? That's right: just 1, for Carlos's marbles. So let's draw 1 unit bar to the right. And do we make it a little tiny unit bar? No, we do not! We have just 1 variable, so let's draw 1 large unit bar, right?*

STEP FIVE—A: *Let's read the first sentence. "Carlos has 8 marbles in his backpack." What does the sentence tell us? Great! It tells us that Carlos has 8 total marbles. Let's go down to the unit bar. Where will we write the total? Sure. Let's write it at the end of the unit bar, to the right.*

B

"If he takes them out and divides them into 4 equal groups, . . ."

Carlos's marbles

8

C

". . . how many marbles will be in each group?"

STEP SIX: *Put the question mark in place.*

Carlos's marbles

8

?

STEP SEVEN: *Work computation to the side or underneath.*

Carlos's marbles

8

?

4 units = 8
8 ÷ 4 = 2
1 unit = 2

B: *Let's move on to the second sentence. Do you see the comma? Let's read that far and pause. "If he takes them out and divides them into 4 equal groups, . . ." We can stop there and show on our unit bar the information we have so far. What does the information indicate we need to do? What should we do to our unit bar to show that we're dividing the marbles equally among 4 groups? You're right! We need to divide our unit bar into 4 equal parts, or fourths. Our unit bar now shows Carlos has a total of 8 marbles, and that total is divided into 4 equal parts.*

C: *Let's go back to the second sentence and pick up after the comma: ". . . how many marbles will be in each group?" What do you notice? Great! It asks our question.*

STEP SIX: *What are we being asked to do? We need to compute how many marbles will go in each of the 4 groups. Where should we put the question mark? Remember, when we're dividing, we're also talking about equal parts, so when I figure out how many are in 1 part, I know how many are in each equal part, correct? So let's put the question mark in the first equal section of our unit bar. Whenever we divide and we want to know the value of 1 of the parts, this is how we show the question mark. We write it in 1 of the equal sections of the unit bar.*

STEP SEVEN: *How are we going to solve this problem? What's the only number you see in our drawing? 8? Terrific! And what are we going to do with it? We're going to go below the problem and divide 8 by 4. Why 4? That's right: because we have 4 equal parts! And if 4 units equal 8, then 1 unit equals what? 2? Great! So how many marbles will there be in each group? 2!*

HOLD THIS THOUGHT

☞ Show division by segmenting the unit bar into equal parts. If the problem asks for the value of one of the parts, place the question mark in one of the segments.

STEP EIGHT: *Answer the question in a complete sentence.*

There will be 2 marbles in each group.

STEP EIGHT: *How should this question be answered? That's right: in a complete sentence! "There will be 2 marbles in each group."*

MILKING THE PROBLEM FOR ALL IT'S WORTH

▶ What if Carlos wanted to divide his marbles into 5 equal groups? How many would there be in each group?

▶ What if he wanted only 2 groups? How many marbles would go in each one if the groups were still equal?

8

DIVISION

During summer camp 176 students were split into groups. If the students were split into 8 equal groups, how many students were put in each group?

" Teacher Talk "

STEP ONE: *Read the entire problem.*

"During summer camp 176 students were split into groups. If the students were split into 8 equal groups, how many students were put in each group?

STEP ONE: *Let's read the problem.*

STEP TWO: *Decide who is involved in the problem.*

students

STEP TWO: *Who is involved in the problem? Do we have anything more specific than just "students"? No, we don't! We need to put 1 variable down on our paper: "students."*

STEP THREE: *Decide what is involved in the problem.*

STEP THREE: *Now that we have our "who" determined, we need to figure out the "what." Is the problem about the students and their socks? Their money? Their pets? No! There is no specific "what" to match the "who." Therefore we just skip Step Three and move on to Step Four.*

STEP FOUR: *Draw unit bars of equal length.*

students

STEP FOUR: *Since we have only 1 variable, we need to draw 1 large bar that can be split up into several segments.*

STEP FIVE: *Read each sentence, one at a time.*

A

"During summer camp 176 students were split into groups."

students   176

STEP FIVE—A: *Let's read the first sentence. "During summer camp 176 students were split into groups." Given that we have our label "students," where would the number 176 be placed in this particular problem? Let's put the number at the end of the bar. We won't put the number inside the bar this time because once the bar is divided up into segments, a number inside the bar would not be accurately displayed in the drawing.*

B

"If the students were split into 8 equal groups, . . ."

students

176

C

". . . how many students were put in each group?"

STEP SIX: *Put the question mark in place.*

students

?							

176

B: Now for the next sentence: "If the students were split into 8 equal groups, . . ." We pause here because of the what? The comma! At this point, what can we do with our 1 large bar? Great! Split the bar into 8 equal pieces. We can do this by splitting the bar in half, or 2 equal pieces. Then take the 2 bars and split each one into 2 equal pieces, creating 4 pieces. Finally, split each of the 4 pieces in half to create 8 equal pieces.

C: Let's continue: ". . . how many students were put in each group?" We have now arrived at the question mark in the problem, so we need to determine where it should be positioned.

STEP SIX: *Where should the question mark be placed? That's right: let's put the question mark in 1 unit.*

HOLD THIS THOUGHT

☞ To split a unit bar into 8 equal pieces, split the bar in half, or 2 equal pieces. Then take the 2 segments and split each one into 2 equal pieces, creating 4 pieces. Finally, split each of the 4 pieces in half to create 8 equal pieces. This helps with drawing to scale and also with estimating.

STEP SEVEN: *Work computation to the side or underneath.*

students

?							176

$8 \text{ units} = 176$

$160 \div 8 = 20$
$16 \div 8 = 2$
$20 + 2 = 22$

OR

$$8 \overline{)176}$$
$$\underline{-16}$$
$$16$$
$$\underline{-16}$$
$$0$$

with quotient 22

OR

$$8 \overline{)17_1 6_0}$$

with quotient 2 2

$1 \text{ unit} = 22$

STEP EIGHT: *Answer the question in a complete sentence.*

At the summer camp, 22 students were put in each group.

STEP SEVEN: What's the only number you see in our drawing? Great! Now we have to figure out what to do with that 176. There are several different ways to solve this particular problem. We know that 176 equals how many units? Great! So we need to split the 176 into 8 equal parts. Based on the mental-math strategy of breaking a number into parts, we can break 176 into 160 and 16. Then we can divide both numbers by 8, resulting in 20 plus 2, or 22.

What would be another way to handle this division? Yes, we could use the traditional algorithm. In that case we would get to the answer of 22 by dividing, multiplying, subtracting, and bringing down, then repeating the process.

Could we also use short division to solve this problem? Absolutely! How would we show that? Yes, like this. By the way, notice how the numbers are in subscript form in the dividend. That's how we do short division. So we know that if 8 units equal 176, then 1 unit equals 22.

STEP EIGHT: Who can answer the question in a complete sentence? "At the summer camp, 22 students were put in each group."

MILKING THE PROBLEM FOR ALL IT'S WORTH

⟹ **If the students were put into 16 equal groups, what would be the total number of students in each group?**

⟹ **What number represents half of the students at summer camp?**

MIXED OPERATIONS (+ & −)

At the start of the day, Jennifer and Maria have the same amount of money. Maria spends $30, and Jennifer gains an additional $25 by working. At the end of the day, how much more money does Jennifer have than Maria?

STEP ONE: *Read the entire problem.*

"At the start of the day, Jennifer and Maria have the same amount of money. Maria spends $30, and Jennifer gains an additional $25 by working. At the end of the day, how much more money does Jennifer have than Maria?"

STEP TWO: *Decide who is involved in the problem.*

Jennifer

Maria

STEP THREE: *Decide what is involved in the problem.*

Jennifer's
money

Maria's
money

STEP FOUR: *Draw unit bars of equal length.*

Jennifer's
money

Maria's
money

" Teacher Talk "

STEP ONE: *Let's read the problem.*

STEP TWO: *Who's involved? Jennifer and Maria are the people involved in the problem. We need to list their names.*

STEP THREE: *What are we talking about? We're talking about money earned or lost by Jennifer and Maria. We write "money" below Jennifer's name and again below Maria's name, so it says "Jennifer's money" and "Maria's money."*

STEP FOUR: *How many unit bars do we need to draw? How many variables are present in this problem? Let's draw a unit bar next to "Jennifer's money" and a unit bar next to "Maria's money."*

STEP FIVE: *Read each sentence, one at a time.*

A

"At the start of the day, Jennifer and Maria have the same amount of money."

B

"Maria spends $30, . . ."

Jennifer's
money

Maria's
money

$30

C

". . . and Jennifer gains an additional $25 by working."

Jennifer's
money

$25

Maria's
money

$30

STEP FIVE—A: *Let's read the first sentence: "At the start of the day, Jennifer and Maria have the same amount of money." Who are we talking about in this sentence? Right: Jennifer and Maria. Who has more money? Which bar should be longer? After looking at the sentence, we realize that Jennifer and Maria have equal amounts of money and that the bars should be the same length. That's what we're already showing, so we're ready to go on to sentence two.*

B: *"Maria spends $30, and Jennifer gains an additional $25 by working." What is the problem with this sentence? It contains too much information! What should we do? We need to break it down into smaller parts. If there is more than one number given in a sentence, we can work the problem one number at a time. So let's read it again and stop after the first number: "Maria spends $30, . . ." What should we do with Maria's bar? Is she gaining more money? Is she losing money? She's spending money, so she's losing money. What should happen to her bar? Great! Remember that with subtraction, we cut a segment of the unit bar and label it. We'll label this one "$30." Once again, we'll put a diagonal slash mark through that segment.*

C: *Let's continue with the sentence: ". . . and Jennifer gains an additional $25 by working." Who are we talking about now? Yes, Jennifer. Should we subtract from Jennifer's bar? Why? What should we do to her bar? Should we add to her unit bar or take away from it? Yes, we'll add a bar of $25 to Jennifer's original unit bar. Her 2 bars should be touching each other. And how big should the new bar be? That's right. Make sure that the bar of $25 is not larger than the bar of $30 that we subtracted from Maria's earnings. We always want to keep the bars proportional because that helps us to solve the problem.*

HOLD THIS THOUGHT

☞ Unit bars need to be proportional. Make sure that the bar of $25 is not larger than the bar of $30.

D

"At the end of the day, how much more money does Jennifer have than Maria?"

STEP SIX: *Put the question mark in place.*

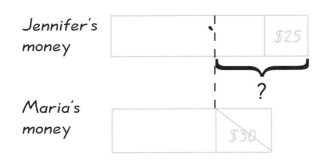

STEP SEVEN: *Work computation to the side or underneath.*

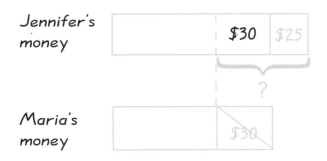

$25 + $30 = $55

D: *Let's continue: "At the end of the day, how much more money does Jennifer have than Maria?" Now that we are at the question, we are ready to go to Step Six.*

STEP SIX: *Notice what the question is asking us to do: find how much more money Jennifer has than Maria. We need to draw a dotted line through Jennifer's bar and down to the end of the bar that shows how much Maria now has. We draw a brace below Jennifer's unit bar from the dotted line to the end of Jennifer's money. Then we place the question mark under the brace. This is the "more" money.*

Notice the parts that are equal. Those are the ones that let us determine how much more money Jennifer has than Maria.

Do we need to know how much money they each started with? No. Why not? That is extraneous information.

STEP SEVEN: *After seeing the drawing, we know that the dotted-line segment of Jennifer's money is worth $30, so let's fill that in. Now we can determine that we have to add the $25 and the $30 to figure out the answer to this problem. We compute to get a sum of $55.*

HOLD THESE THOUGHTS

☞ Draw a dotted line between unit bars to point out segments of equal value.

☞ Don't get distracted looking for extraneous information. Focus on what's needed to solve the problem.

STEP EIGHT: *Answer the question in a complete sentence.*

At the end of the day, Jennifer has $55 more than Maria.

STEP EIGHT: *How can we answer the question? "At the end of the day, Jennifer has $55 more than Maria." Great!*

MILKING THE PROBLEM FOR ALL IT'S WORTH

▯▶ If Maria hadn't spent the $30, how much money would she need to earn in order to match Jennifer's total money in the end?

▯▶ Can we determine what the original bars drawn are worth? Why or why not?

MIXED OPERATIONS (+ & –)

Phil's goal was to score 36 points during basketball practice this week. If he scored 8 points on Monday, 8 on Tuesday, 6 on Wednesday, and 8 on Thursday, how many more points does he need to score on Friday to reach his goal?

STEP ONE: *Read the entire problem.*

"Phil's goal was to score 36 points during basketball practice this week. If he scored 8 points on Monday, 8 on Tuesday, 6 on Wednesday, and 8 on Thursday, how many more points does he need to score on Friday to reach his goal?"

STEP TWO: *Decide who is involved in the problem.*

Phil

STEP THREE: *Decide what is involved in the problem.*

Phil's points on Monday

Phil's points on Tuesday

Phil's points on Wednesday

Phil's points on Thursday

Phil's points on Friday

" Teacher Talk "

STEP ONE: *Let's read the entire problem and picture what this problem is about.*

STEP TWO: *Who is involved in this problem? Yes, Phil is involved. Let's write his name on the left, below the problem.*

STEP THREE: *Now that we know Phil is involved in this problem, we need to figure out Phil's what? What are we talking about? Are we talking about Phil's shoes? His cookies? We're talking about Phil's points. Great! We are trying to figure out how many points it will take for Phil to make his goal. Let's write the word "points" next to Phil's name. Why do we add an apostrophe and an "s"? That's it! We want to show the points belong to Phil.*

But what else do we know about Phil's points? Were they all scored on the same day? No. So how many labels do we need? That's right: 5. Why? Right again! We need 1 label for Phil's points for each day. So what should our labels say? Yes!

STEP FOUR: Draw unit bars of equal length.

Phil's points
on Monday ☐

Phil's points
on Tuesday ☐

Phil's points
on Wednesday ☐

Phil's points
on Thursday ☐

Phil's points
on Friday ☐

STEP FOUR: *Now that we've determined who and what we're talking about, let's draw a unit bar for each variable in our problem.*

STEP FIVE: Read each sentence, one at a time.

A

"Phil's goal was to score 36 points during basketball practice this week."

Phil's points
on Monday ☐

Phil's points
on Tuesday ☐

Phil's points
on Wednesday ☐ } 36

Phil's points
on Thursday ☐

Phil's points
on Friday ☐

STEP FIVE—A: *Are you ready to read the first sentence? "Phil's goal was to score 36 points during basketball practice this week." How will we record this information on our drawing? Great! The total Phil wants to score is 36, so we'll write that number to the right with a brace to show that 36 is the total for all of the days.*

HOLD THIS THOUGHT

☞ Use a brace to indicate the total for multiple unit bars.

B

"If he scored 8 points on Monday, . . ."

Phil's points on Monday	8
Phil's points on Tuesday	
Phil's points on Wednesday	
Phil's points on Thursday	
Phil's points on Friday	

} 36

B: Let's go on to the second sentence: "If he scored 8 points on Monday, . . ." There's a comma, so let's stop and show in the appropriate unit bar the information we have so far. Where will we write the 8? That's right: it will go in the unit bar for "Phil's points on Monday."

C

" . . . 8 on Tuesday, . . ."

Phil's points on Monday	8
Phil's points on Tuesday	8
Phil's points on Wednesday	
Phil's points on Thursday	
Phil's points on Friday	

} 36

C: We need to go back to the second sentence and continue from where we left off: ". . . 8 on Tuesday, . . ." What do we do at a comma? Yes, we'll pause. And we'll go down and add this information to our Tuesday unit bar.

HOLD THIS THOUGHT

☞ If there is more than one number given in a sentence, work the problem one number at a time.

D

" . . . 6 on Wednesday, . . ."

Phil's points on Monday	8	
Phil's points on Tuesday	8	
Phil's points on Wednesday	6	36
Phil's points on Thursday		
Phil's points on Friday		

D: *Ready to continue? Let's go back to the second sentence and pick up where we left off: ". . . 6 on Wednesday, . . ." Another comma. What do we do with this information? Great! We write it in the Wednesday unit bar. But we have a problem, don't we? What's our problem? That's right: this unit bar is worth 6, and each of the bars before it is worth 8. Should all 3 unit bars be the same size? No! Is 6 greater than or less than 8? That's right: 6 is less than 8. So should the unit bar for 6 be shorter or longer than the unit bar for 8? That's right: shorter. So let's mark off a segment of the unit bar for Wednesday and let's draw a diagonal slash through it to show that we're getting rid of that piece. Now are the bars the right size so far? Yes!*

E

" . . . and 8 on Thursday, . . ."

Phil's points on Monday	8	
Phil's points on Tuesday	8	
Phil's points on Wednesday	6	36
Phil's points on Thursday	8	
Phil's points on Friday		

E: *Are we finished with the second sentence? No, we are not. There's still more! Let's return to the place we left off again: ". . . and 8 on Thursday, . . ." How will we list this information? Great! We'll add the 8 to the Thursday unit bar. Do we need to do anything to its size? Why or why not? Right: it's fine the way it is because all of the unit bars that are worth 8 are the same size.*

HOLD THIS THOUGHT

☞ You can always adjust the size of a unit bar as you learn more information. When you lengthen the bar, it means you're adding, and when you shorten the bar, you're subtracting.

F

" . . . how many more points does he need to score on Friday to reach his goal?"

STEP SIX: *Put the question mark in place.*

Phil's points on Monday	8
Phil's points on Tuesday	8
Phil's points on Wednesday	6
Phil's points on Thursday	8
Phil's points on Friday	**?**

} 36

STEP SEVEN: *Work computation to the side or underneath.*

Phil's points on Monday	8
Phil's points on Tuesday	8
Phil's points on Wednesday	6
Phil's points on Thursday	8
Phil's points on Friday	?

} 36

$$8 + 8 + 6 + 8 = 30 \quad OR \quad (3 \times 8) + 6 = 30$$

$$36 - 30 = 6$$

F: *Let's read the rest of the second sentence: ". . . how many more points does he need to score on Friday to reach his goal?" What do you notice? Great! It becomes our question. Let's go to the next step.*

STEP SIX: *What are we being asked to solve? We're asked to determine how many more points Phil needs to score on Friday to reach his goal. Let's look at the unit bars. We have numbers in the bars for Monday, Tuesday, Wednesday, and Thursday. Do we have a number for Friday? No. Does that bar represent the question that's being asked? Is that where our question mark should go? Absolutely!*

STEP SEVEN: *How are we going to solve this problem? What is the total number of points Phil wants to score? How can we figure out how many points Phil has scored so far? We could add. Does anyone see another way of figuring out how many points he has scored from Monday through Thursday? Great! There are 3 groups of 8 in our unit bars. We can multiply them and then add 6 to that total. Let's show our work below the problem. We have an answer, but have we answered the question that's in the problem? No, we have not.*

The question asks how many more points Phil needs to score on Friday to reach his goal. What do we need to do next? Great! We need to take the 30 points Phil has scored so far and subtract them from his goal of 36. We again show our work below the problem. What is the difference? 6? Right!

Now, before we can answer the question, we need to make sure our drawing is showing the problem correctly. Does anybody see a problem with the drawing? That's right! The unit bar with the question mark isn't the right size. What does that unit bar represent? What value? That's right: 6. So do we need to shorten it or lengthen it? That's right: we need to shorten it. So let's do exactly what we did with the bar for Wednesday: we'll mark off a segment and put a slash through it. Why do we do that? Yes, to show that the 6 points for Friday are worth less than the 8 points on Thursday.

STEP EIGHT: *Answer the question in a complete sentence.*

Phil needs to score 6 points on Friday to reach his goal.

STEP EIGHT: *How should this question be answered? Who can give me a complete sentence? Great! "Phil needs to score 6 points on Friday to reach his goal."*

MILKING THE PROBLEM FOR ALL IT'S WORTH

▥▶ If Phil scored 10 points on Friday, how many points over his goal would he score?

▥▶ If Phil scored only 4 points on Friday, by how many points would he miss his goal?

▥▶ What is the average number of points Phil scored each day of basketball practice?

MULTIPLICATION

Cheryl bought a carton of large beads. She divided the beads evenly among 8 boxes, so that each box contained 25 beads. How many beads did she have altogether?

....

STEP ONE: *Read the entire problem.*

"Cheryl bought a carton of large beads. She divided the beads evenly among 8 boxes, so that each box contained 25 beads. How many beads did she have altogether?"

STEP TWO: *Decide who is involved in the problem.*

Cheryl

STEP THREE: *Decide what is involved in the problem.*

Cheryl's
beads

STEP FOUR: *Draw unit bars of equal length.*

Cheryl's
beads

STEP FIVE: *Read each sentence, one at a time.*
A

"Cheryl bought a carton of large beads."

Cheryl's
beads

" Teacher Talk "

STEP ONE: *Let's read the entire problem and picture what it is about.*

STEP TWO: *Who is involved in this problem? We're talking about Cheryl, so let's write her name on the left, below the problem.*

STEP THREE: *Now, what are we talking about? Cheryl's what? Great! We're talking about her beads. Let's add "beads," so we now have identified "Cheryl's beads."*

STEP FOUR: *We have determined we're talking about Cheryl's beads. How many variables do we have? Not how many beads, but how many variables. That's right: just 1. So we need to draw 1 large unit bar.*

STEP FIVE—A: *Let's begin solving the problem by reading just the first sentence. "Cheryl bought a carton of large beads." Do you see how we have already illustrated this information with the unit bar?*

B

"She divided the beads evenly among 8 boxes, . . ."

Cheryl's beads

B: *Let's now go on to the second sentence: "She divided the beads evenly among 8 boxes, . . ." There's a comma, so let's stop and illustrate just this information. If we go to our unit bar, how can we show that the beads are divided evenly among 8 boxes? That's right: we divide our unit bar into 8 equal parts.*

C

" . . . so that each box contained 25 beads."

Cheryl's beads

25	25	25	25	25	25	25	25

C: *Let's pick up where we left off in the second sentence: ". . . so that each box contained 25 beads." If we go to our unit bar, how can we show that each box contained 25 beads? How many boxes does Cheryl have? And how many beads are in each box? Can we write "25" in each of the 8 boxes? Great!*

D

"How many beads did she have altogether?"

D: *Let's continue: "How many beads did she have altogether?" That brings us to the question.*

STEP SIX: *Put the question mark in place.*

Cheryl's beads

| 25 | 25 | 25 | 25 | 25 | 25 | 25 | 25 | **?**
|---|---|---|---|---|---|---|---|

STEP SIX: *What does this question tell us we need to do? You're correct: we need to find the total number of beads. Let's write the question mark to the right of the unit bar.*

STEP SEVEN: *Work computation to the side or underneath.*

Cheryl's beads

| 25 | 25 | 25 | 25 | 25 | 25 | 25 | 25 | ?
|---|---|---|---|---|---|---|---|

25 + 25 + 25 + 25 + 25 + 25 + 25 + 25 = 200

OR

8 X 25 = 200

OR

4 X 25 = 100
100 X 2 = 200

STEP SEVEN: *Now we're ready to solve the problem. What numbers do we have in our drawing? That's right. So now, give me a suggestion for finding the total. Sure! We could add 25 eight times. Let's show our work below the problem. Now is there another way we can solve this? Yes! We can multiply 8 times 25. Anybody else? Yes, we could say 4 X 25 and then multiply the answer by 2. What is the answer? You're right! No matter how you solve the problem, the answer is still 200.*

HOLD THIS THOUGHT

☞ No matter how you calculate it, the answer is the same! This is very important for students to see.

Cheryl had 200 beads altogether.

MILKING THE PROBLEM FOR ALL IT'S WORTH

➤ If Cheryl had 10 boxes, what would be her total number of beads?

➤ If each of the 8 boxes had 27 beads, how many would Cheryl have altogether?

➤ If she gave away 6 of the boxes, how many beads would Cheryl have left?

FRACTIONS

There were 80 air conditioners at a local warehouse. If 3/5 of the air conditioners were sold during one day when the heat was overwhelming, how many air conditioners were left for sale after that day?

....

"Teacher Talk"

STEP ONE: *Read the entire problem.*

"There were 80 air conditioners at a local warehouse. If 3/5 of the air conditioners were sold during one day when the heat was overwhelming, how many air conditioners were left for sale after that day?"

STEP TWO: *Decide who is involved in the problem.*

STEP THREE: *Decide what is involved in the problem.*

air
conditioners

STEP FOUR: *Draw unit bars of equal length.*

air .
conditioners

STEP ONE: *Let's read the problem.*

STEP TWO: *Who are we talking about? Is there a person involved in this problem? Do we need to list a person for this problem? No. Therefore we can skip right to Step Three.*

STEP THREE: *Since there are no "whos," we need to clearly define our "whats." In this case, what is the "what"? We write the "what" as "air conditioners."*

STEP FOUR: *We have only 1 variable, so we need to draw 1 unit bar. And let's make it a large one. Since we're working with fractions, we know that eventually we're going to split that bar up into parts. It makes sense to make a large bar so that we'll be able to see the parts clearly.*

HOLD THIS THOUGHT

☞ When working with fractions and just one variable, begin with a large unit bar so you can see the parts clearly.

STEP FIVE: Read each sentence, one at a time.

A

"There were 80 air conditioners at a local warehouse."

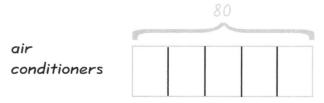

air
conditioners

B

"If 3/5 of the air conditioners were sold during one day when the heat was overwhelming, . . ."

air
conditioners

C

". . . how many air conditioners were left for sale after that day?"

air
conditioners

STEP SIX: Put the question mark in place.

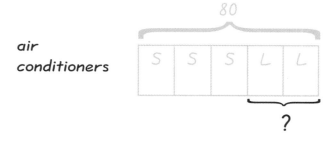

air
conditioners

STEP FIVE—A: Let's read the first sentence. "There were 80 air conditioners at a local warehouse." We can label the whole bar with the number 80. Instead of putting the number inside the bar as we sometimes do, let's put it above the bar, with a brace. We know we need to break the bar into what? Into parts. If we put the 80 above the bar, then it won't be in the way when we want to write inside the bar later. We could put the total above the bar, below the bar, or to the right. Any of those ways is correct.

B: Let's read the next sentence up to the comma: "If 3/5 of the air conditioners were sold during 1 day when the heat was overwhelming, . . ." How many parts should we split our bar into? Which part of the fraction tells us to do that? What do we call the bottom number in a fraction? The denominator? Right!

Should all 5 pieces be of equal size? Yes! Why?

C: Now for the final question: ". . . how many air conditioners were left for sale after that day?" Before we can find out how many air conditioners were left, we need to label 3 of the bars with the letter "S" for sold. That way we can get ready to put our question mark where it belongs. And how should we label the other 2 bars to show that they're left? With an "L" in each? Perfect!

STEP SIX: Since we want to know what was left, where do we put the question mark? Yes, we need to put a brace below the last 2 units and put a question mark in place for this particular problem.

HOLD THIS THOUGHT

☛ If the question asks for the value of two or more of the parts, draw a brace to connect those two parts and place the question mark outside the brace.

STEP SEVEN: *Work computation to the side or underneath.*

air conditioners

80				
S	S	S	L	L
16	16	16	16	16

?

5 units = 80

$$5 \overline{)80} = 16$$

1 unit = 16

16 X 2 = 32

STEP EIGHT: *Answer the question in a complete sentence.*

There were 32 air conditioners left for sale at the local warehouse after the hot day.

STEP SEVEN: *Now we can solve the problem. What is the only number that you see in the drawing? That is correct! The only number shown is 80. If 80 is the value of the whole unit bar, how many fractional parts is that 80 divided into? Yes, 5! So if 5 units are worth 80, how much is each individual unit worth? 16? Yes!*

Now, of those 5 parts, how many were sold? 3 is correct. How many parts are we interested in? 2? Great work!

Take 16 and multiply it by 2, or simply double the 16.

STEP EIGHT: *And the answer, in a complete sentence, is . . . ? "There were 32 air conditioners left for sale at the local warehouse after the hot day."*

MILKING THE PROBLEM FOR ALL IT'S WORTH

⟿   How many air conditioners were sold?

⟿   What fraction of the original air conditioners were left to be sold?

⟿   How many more air conditioners were sold than not sold?

FRACTIONS

Abu earned $30 mowing lawns on Saturday. He spent half of the money on a new CD, and he spent 1/3 of the remaining money on lunch. Does he have enough money to also buy a bike attachment that costs $12.98?

··

STEP ONE: *Read the entire problem.*

"Abu earned $30 mowing lawns on Saturday. He spent half of the money on a new CD, and he spent 1/3 of the remaining money on lunch. Does he have enough money to also buy a bike attachment that costs $12.98?"

STEP TWO: *Decide who is involved in the problem.*

Abu

STEP THREE: *Decide what is involved in the problem.*

Abu's
money

STEP FOUR: *Draw unit bars of equal length.*

Abu's
money

" Teacher Talk "

STEP ONE: *Let's read the entire problem to get a picture of what it's about.*

STEP TWO: *Before we begin deciding who and what we are talking about, let's look once again at the problem. This problem has a special word in it: the word "remaining." We have a rule for that word. The rule is that when we see the word "remaining" or "remainder," that's a clue that it will begin with 1 large unit bar. So before we go any further, let's underline the word "remaining" in our problem to remind us of that rule.*

Now, let's go through our steps: Who is involved in this problem? Who are we talking about? That's right: we're talking about Abu. We need to write "Abu" on the left, below the problem.

STEP THREE: *Next, what are we talking about? Abu's what? His CD? His lunch? His marbles? His homework? His what? Correct! We're talking about Abu's money. We need to add "money" below "Abu" so that we see "Abu's money."*

STEP FOUR: *How many variables are we talking about? Just 1. What did we say we were going to do so far as unit bars were concerned in this problem? That's right! Since the word "remaining" appears in this problem, we need to draw 1 large unit bar. Let's draw it next to "Abu's money."*

STEP FIVE: *Read each sentence, one at a time.*

A

"Abu earned $30 mowing lawns on Saturday."

B

"He spent half of the money on a new CD, . . ."

C

". . . and he spent 1/3 of the <u>remaining</u> money on lunch."

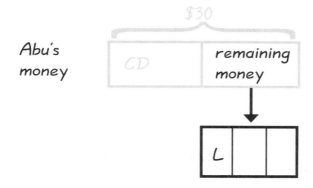

HOLD THIS THOUGHT

☛ In a "remainder" problem, the unit bar that you bring down needs to be the same size as the segment of the first bar that it represents.

STEP FIVE—A: *Now we can begin illustrating the problem. Let's read the first sentence. "Abu earned $30 mowing lawns on Saturday." How should we illustrate the information from this sentence? Great! Abu earned a total of $30, so let's show this total above the unit bar, with a brace.*

B: *Let's continue with the second sentence. "He spent half of the money on a new CD, . . ." There's a comma, so we need to stop. What can we do to the unit bar to show Abu spent half of his money on a CD? You're right: we can divide the unit bar in half. Why not thirds? Why not fourths? You've got it. The problem tells us half! What did he spend half of his money buying? A CD. Great! Where can we write this label? Good! Show it in the first half of the unit bar.*

C: *Let's go on: ". . . and he spent 1/3 of the remaining money on lunch." Where is the remaining money? Is it the money Abu spent on a CD? No. It's the money remaining after Abu bought the CD. It's half of the $30. How can we label that? Let's write "remaining money" in that segment of the unit bar.*

Watch as I show you how we're going to model this information. We're going to add a second step in which we work only with the remaining money. We want to bring down the remainder. How much of the unit bar will I bring down? Great! We'll bring down just half.

Underneath our original unit bar, let's draw an arrow and repeat half of the first unit bar. Watch how big I make this new unit bar. Does this half of the unit bar represent the entire $30 Abu earned mowing lawns? No. What does it represent? Great! It represents half of the $30. It's the money remaining after he bought the CD. Remember, the new unit bar needs to go right under the "remaining money" in the first unit bar and it needs to be the same size as that segment.

Now we can continue. How can we show that Abu spent 1/3 of the remaining money on lunch? Great! We divide this new unit bar into thirds. How many thirds did Abu spend on lunch? That's correct: 1/3. Let's write "L" for "lunch" in the first third of this unit bar.

D

"Does he have enough money to also buy a bike attachment that costs $12.98?"

STEP SIX: *Put the question mark in place.*

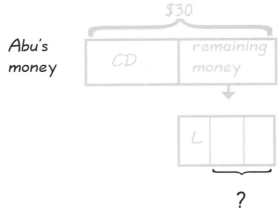

(Is this amount greater than $12.98, the amount needed to buy the attachment?)

STEP SEVEN: *Work computation to the side or underneath.*

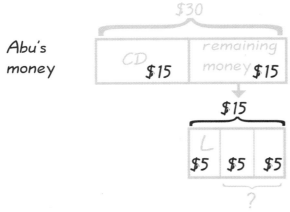

(Is this amount greater than $12.98, the amount needed to buy the attachment?)

2 units = $30	3 units = $15
$30 ÷ 2 = $15	$15 ÷ 3 = $5
1 unit = $15	1 unit = $5
	$5 X 2 = $10

D: *Let's read the rest of the problem: "Does he have enough money to also buy a bike attachment that costs $12.98?" That brings us to the what? To the question.*

STEP SIX: *In this step, we have to put the question mark in place. What must we do to figure out if Abu will have enough money for the attachment? You're right: we need to compute how much money he has after he's bought his lunch. Let's draw a brace under the last two-thirds of the bottom unit bar and place our question mark there. Since we are being asked more than how much money he had left, let's write a question next to the question mark. This type of problem requires you to make a judgment. It does not simply ask you for an answer.*

STEP SEVEN: *We are now ready to do our computations. Where should we begin? Let's start with the first unit bar, the one we divided in half. What's the only number you see with that unit bar? If Abu earned a total of $30, how can we figure out the value of each half? Great! We know that 2 units equal $30, so we divide 30 by 2 and see that 1 unit equals $15. Let's show the work below this problem. What's our answer? $15. It's time to label. How much did the CD cost? $15. We'll label the CD half "$15." What does the other half represent? His remaining money. Good! Let's label that half "$15" also.*

Let's continue. Follow the arrow down to the portion of the unit bar that represents Abu's remaining money. How much total remaining money does Abu have? Great! He has $15. Where should we write the total? Let's put it above the unit bar, again using a brace. We can write $15 there to show Abu's total remaining money.

Let's move on with the computation. What does the unit bar show we did with Abu's remaining money? Did we divide it in half? No. Did we divide it into fifths? No. We divided it into thirds. Why? So now we know that 3 units equal $15. How can we figure out the value of each third? Yes, we can divide $15 by 3. Let's show our work below the problem. What's our answer?

Yes, 1 unit is worth $5. Let's label each third as $5. So, how much money did Abu spend on lunch? $5 is correct. But is that the question we're being asked? No, so let's keep going.

How can we figure out how much money Abu had left after buying lunch? Great! We can multiply $5 X 2 to get a total of $10. Let's show our work below the problem.

STEP EIGHT: Answer the question in a complete sentence.

No, Abu has only $10 left, so he does not have enough money to also buy the bike attachment.

STEP EIGHT: *It's time to answer the question. Notice again that the question does not ask how much money Abu had left. What does it ask us? Yes, it asks if Abu will have enough money left to buy a bike attachment that costs $12.98. Let's think about that. How much money does Abu have left? $10. How much does he need for the attachment? $12.98. Does he have enough money to buy it? No. How can we answer this question? "No, Abu has only $10 left. so he does not have enough money to also buy the bike attachment."*

MILKING THE PROBLEM FOR ALL IT'S WORTH

▐▶ **How much more money will Abu need to buy the attachment?**

▐▶ **How much more money did Abu spend on the CD than on lunch?**

▐▶ **What fraction of $30 is the amount Abu spent on lunch?**

RATE

A car can travel 300 miles on 12 gallons of gas. How far can the car travel on 15 gallons of gas?

STEP ONE: *Read the entire problem.*

"A car can travel 300 miles on 12 gallons of gas. How far can the car travel on 15 gallons of gas?"

STEP TWO: *Decide who is involved in the problem.*

STEP THREE: *Decide what is involved in the problem.*

car's
miles
per
gallon

STEP FOUR: *Draw unit bars of equal length.*

car's
miles
per
gallon

" Teacher Talk "

STEP ONE: *Let's read the problem.*

STEP TWO: *Who's involved? Is a car a person? Is there a specific person involved in this problem? No! No! No! Therefore skip to Step Three.*

STEP THREE: *What is involved in this problem? Yes, a car! Yes, gallons of gas! In a rate problem, we want to label our "what" and also show what kind of units we're working with—our "units per units." In this case, what are we looking for? We want to know what per what? Miles per gallon? Absolutely! So let's make our label say "car's miles per gallon."*

STEP FOUR: *How many variables do we have in the problem? "Only 1" is correct! When we have just 1 variable, how many unit bars do we draw? Right! And how large is it? Yes! We can see that we're going to need to divide this unit bar, so let's make it big!*

HOLD THIS THOUGHT

☛ In a rate problem, label the "what" in terms of "units per units."

STEP FIVE: *Read each sentence, one at a time.*

A

"A car can travel 300 miles . . ."

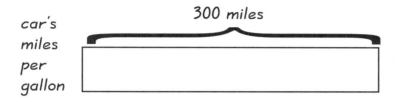

B

". . . on 12 gallons of gas."

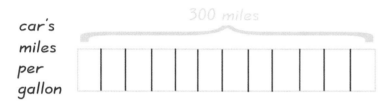

C

car's
miles
per
gallon

STEP FIVE—A: Let's read the first sentence. "A car can travel 300 miles on 12 gallons of gas." Notice that there is a problem with this sentence. What is it? Yes, there is too much information in the sentence. When you see 2 numbers in 1 sentence, that can be an indicator that there is too much information in that sentence. If we break it down, we see the first part says we have a car that travels 300 miles. So we take the unit bar that we've created and add a brace at the top. Then we add "300 miles" above the brace.

B: If we continue, we see that the 300 miles are represented by 12 gallons of gas. What could we do to show that all 300 miles are shared by 12 gallons of gas? Great! Break the bar up into 12 equal segments.

C: Now we need to place a label under each segment to show that we're talking about gallons. With a rate problem, we need to have a double label because rate is "something per something." In this case we're talking about miles per gallon, so our labels are "miles" above the bar and "gal." below each of the individual segments.

HOLD THIS THOUGHT

☞ With a rate problem, you need to have a double label because rate is "something per something."

D

"How far can the car travel on 15 gallons of gas?"

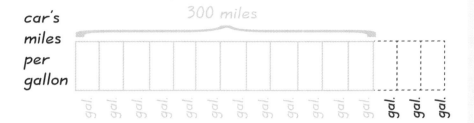

STEP SIX: *Put the question mark in place.*

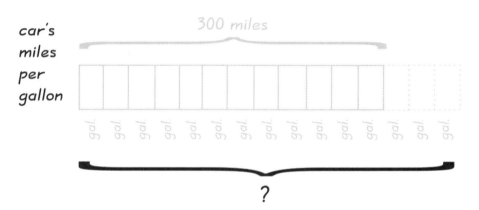

D: *Now let's go to the next sentence, which is already asking us the question: "How far can the car travel on 15 gallons of gas?" We have only 12 gallons shown in the drawing. How can we show 15? Yes, add another 3 units to the end of the original bar of 12, again labeling each one. Now we're ready for the question.*

STEP SIX: *Do we want to know the value of just 1 unit? 12 units? 15 units? How do you know that? What does putting the question mark in place force you to do?*

Correctamundo! Answer the correct question—the one that is being asked. Often students rush through word problems and answer the wrong question in a particular problem. We don't want to do that!

So where do we want to put the question mark in this problem? With rate problems, sometimes it's clearer if we put the question mark above or below the unit bar. So let's put the question mark for the total below the bar, and let's use a brace to make it clear that it represents the total for all 15 units. That is what we are looking for.

HOLD THESE THOUGHTS

☛ Too often, students rush through a problem and answer the wrong question. Placing the question mark helps to prevent that.

☛ Rate problems are sometimes clearer if you label the total above or below the bar, with a brace.

STEP SEVEN: *Work computation to the side or underneath.*

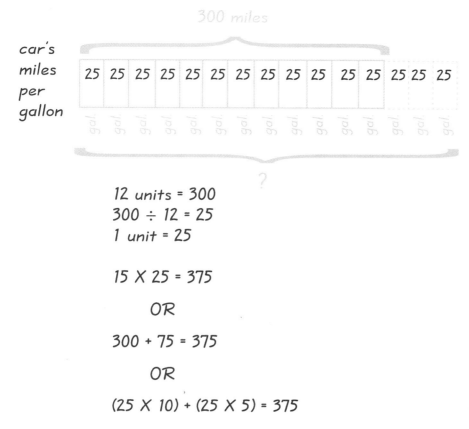

12 units = 300
300 ÷ 12 = 25
1 unit = 25

15 X 25 = 375

OR

300 + 75 = 375

OR

(25 X 10) + (25 X 5) = 375

STEP EIGHT: *Answer the question in a complete sentence.*

The car can travel 375 miles on 15 gallons of gas.

STEP SEVEN: *What is the one number we see in our drawing? Yes, 300! How many units does 300 share? Is it all 15? No, no, no, no. Remember that 300 represented only the first 12 units. So if 12 units equal 300, how do we find what 1 unit is worth? Divide 300 by 12. What do you get?*

Good! Each unit is worth 25. I'll put 25 in each of the first 12 segments. Now, what should we put in the last 3 units? Who said "25 again"? Exactly right!

What should we do to get the total for all 15 units? Multiply 15 by 25? Sure. Are there any other possibilities? Yes, you could take 300 and add 3 times 25, or 75, to equal 375. Any other ideas? Sure. Take 25 and multiply it by 10. Now, take 25 and multiply it by 5. Add the 2 together. The result again is 375. Any way you look at it, the answer is 375!

STEP EIGHT: *How would you answer the question in a complete sentence? "The car can travel 375 miles on 15 gallons of gas."*

MILKING THE PROBLEM FOR ALL IT'S WORTH

▶ **How far could the car travel on 20 gallons of gas?**

▶ **Why is it important in model drawing to find the value of 1 unit?**

RATIO

The ratio of Ty's books to Ling's books is 3 : 4. Ty has 60 books. If Ty buys another 5 books, what will be the new ratio of Ty's books to Ling's books?

....

STEP ONE*: Read the entire problem.*

"The ratio of Ty's books to Ling's books is 3 : 4. Ty has 60 books. If Ty buys another 5 books, what will be the new ratio of Ty's books to Ling's books?"

STEP TWO*: Decide who is involved in the problem.*

Ty

Ling

STEP THREE*: Decide what is involved in the problem.*

Ty's books

Ling's books

STEP FOUR*: Draw unit bars of equal length.*

Ty's books

Ling's books

" Teacher Talk "

STEP ONE*: Let's read the problem.*

STEP TWO*: Who should we list first? Ty, yes! Why should he be listed first? Who should be listed second? Ling, yes! Is there a third variable? No.*

STEP THREE*: What are we talking about? We have Ty's and Ling's what? Books!*

STEP FOUR*: How many bars need to be drawn for this particular problem? How many variables do we have? So we need 2 unit bars, 1 for Ty's books and 1 for Ling's books.*

STEP FIVE: *Read each sentence, one at a time.*

A

"The ratio of Ty's books to Ling's books is 3 : 4."

Ty's books

Ling's books

B

"Ty has 60 books."

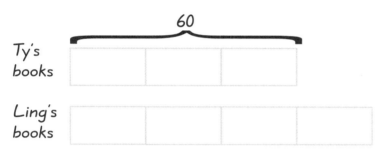

C

"If Ty buys another 5 books, . . ."

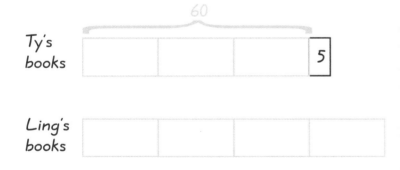

D

". . . what will be the new ratio of Ty's books to Ling's books?"

STEP FIVE—A: *Let's read the first sentence: "The ratio of Ty's books to Ling's books is 3 : 4." At this time, our unit bars show the ratio being 1 : 1. Does the problem ask for the ratio to be 1 : 1? No. This problem asks for 3 : 4. We need how many* more *bars added onto Ty's first bar? Great! The answer is 2. Therefore how many more bars do we need to add to Ling's first bar? Great! The answer is 3.*

We need to make sure all bars are the same size. In this case, we need to make sure Ty's unit bars are the same size as what? The same size as Ling's, so we can compare them.

B: *Let's continue reading: "Ty has 60 books." Where do we need to put the number 60? Let's put a brace over Ty's three units and add a label for "60." We're not putting the 60 at the end because earlier we read that he's going to be getting more. We need to leave room to add more.*

C: *Go on to the next sentence: "If Ty buys another 5 books, . . ." We pause because of what? The comma! And now we add a bar worth 5 to Ty's bars. Is 5 as big as 60? No, so the new bar should be much smaller than what we already have.*

D: *Let's finish that sentence: " . . . what will be the new ratio of Ty's books to Ling's books?" That brings us to Step Six.*

STEP FIVE: *Read each sentence, one at a time.*

A

"The ratio of Ty's books to Ling's books is 3 : 4."

Ty's books

Ling's books

B

"Ty has 60 books."

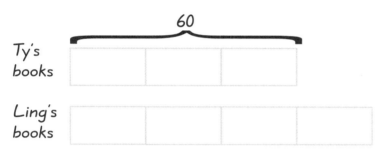

C

"If Ty buys another 5 books, . . ."

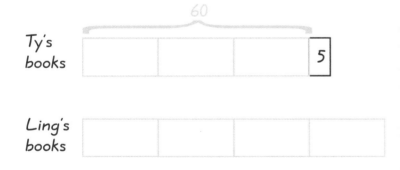

D

". . . what will be the new ratio of Ty's books to Ling's books?"

STEP FIVE—A: *Let's read the first sentence: "The ratio of Ty's books to Ling's books is 3 : 4." At this time, our unit bars show the ratio being 1 : 1. Does the problem ask for the ratio to be 1 : 1? No. This problem asks for 3 : 4. We need how many* more *bars added onto Ty's first bar? Great! The answer is 2. Therefore how many more bars do we need to add to Ling's first bar? Great! The answer is 3.*

We need to make sure all bars are the same size. In this case, we need to make sure Ty's unit bars are the same size as what? The same size as Ling's, so we can compare them.

B: *Let's continue reading: "Ty has 60 books." Where do we need to put the number 60? Let's put a brace over Ty's three units and add a label for "60." We're not putting the 60 at the end because earlier we read that he's going to be getting more. We need to leave room to add more.*

C: *Go on to the next sentence: "If Ty buys another 5 books, . . ." We pause because of what? The comma! And now we add a bar worth 5 to Ty's bars. Is 5 as big as 60? No, so the new bar should be much smaller than what we already have.*

D: *Let's finish that sentence: " . . . what will be the new ratio of Ty's books to Ling's books?" That brings us to Step Six.*

Problems for Guided Practice   73

STEP SIX: **Put the question mark in place.**

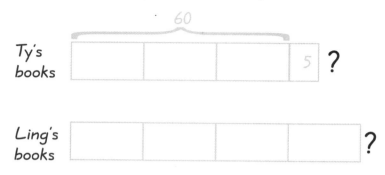

Ty's
books

Ling's
books

STEP SIX: *Since we are dealing with a problem that asks for the ratio of 1 variable to another, we need to put in 2 question marks, 1 for Ty's total and 1 for Ling's total. Now we can compute.*

STEP SEVEN: **Work computation to the side or underneath.**

| | 60 | | 5 | ? |

Ty's
books: 20 | 20 | 20

Ling's
books: 20 | 20 | 20 | 20

3 units = 60
60 ÷ 3 = 20
1 unit = 20

20 + 20 + 20 + 5 = 65
20 + 20 + 20 + 20 = 80
65 : 80

65 ÷ 5 = 13
80 ÷ 5 = 16

13 : 16

STEP SEVEN: *How can we solve this problem? First, we know that the number 60 in our drawing represents how many units? That's right: 3! Therefore we can divide 60 by 3 to get a quotient of 20. So we know that 1 unit equals 20.*

How many units in our drawing are the same size? If we know each of Ty's is worth 20, what do we know about Ling's? Great! So we place "20" in each of our 7 equal units. We now notice that Ty has 20 + 20 + 20 + 5 books and Ling has 20 + 20 + 20 + 20 books. The new ratio appears to be 65 : 80.

Can we leave our answer as 65 : 80? What can we do to give a better answer? Let's simplify! So how do we simplify? That's right! Divide both the 65 and the 80 by the greatest common factor to reach the new answer. What's the greatest common factor? 5? Right! Do we get 13 : 16 as the new ratio? We sure do!

HOLD THIS THOUGHT

☛ When dealing with a problem that asks for the ratio of one variable to another, use two question marks.

STEP EIGHT: *Answer the question in a complete sentence.*

The new ratio of Ty's books to Ling's books will be 13 : 16.

STEP EIGHT: *How would you answer the question in a complete sentence? "The new ratio of Ty's books to Ling's books will be 13 : 16."*

MILKING THE PROBLEM FOR ALL IT'S WORTH

▐▌▶ **What is the fraction that would represent Ty's books relative to the total of Ty's books plus Ling's books?**

▐▌▶ **Suppose that instead of 5 books, Ty buys another 15 books. What would be the new ratio of Ty's books to Ling's books?**

ADDITION & SUBTRACTION OF DECIMALS

Pedro purchased 5 shirts and 3 pairs of pants at the department store. All the shirts were the same price, and each pair of pants cost $1.20 more than each shirt. If Pedro spent $163.60 on all of the shirts and pants, how much did each shirt cost?

STEP ONE: *Read the entire problem.*

"Pedro purchased 5 shirts and 3 pairs of pants at the department store. All the shirts were the same price, and each pair of pants cost $1.20 more than each shirt. If Pedro spent $163.60 on all of the shirts and pants, how much did each shirt cost?"

STEP TWO: *Decide who is involved in the problem.*

Pedro

STEP THREE: *Decide what is involved in the problem.*

Pedro's shirts

Pedro's pants

STEP ONE: *Let's read the problem.*

STEP TWO: *Who's involved in this problem? How many people are involved in this problem? How many variables do we have thus far?*

STEP THREE: *We know we are dealing with Pedro in this problem. What is it about Pedro that we need to be concerned with? Yes, his shirts and pants. We have 2 variables. We need to list the variables as Pedro's shirts and Pedro's pants.*

STEP FOUR: Draw unit bars of equal length.

Pedro's
shirts

Pedro's
pants

STEP FIVE: Read each sentence, one at a time.

A

"Pedro purchased 5 shirts . . ."

Pedro's
shirts

Pedro's
pants

B

". . . and 3 pairs of pants at the department store."

Pedro's
shirts

Pedro's
pants

C

"All the shirts were the same price, . . ."

STEP FOUR: *Since we have 2 variables, how many unit bars do we need? That's right: 2.*

STEP FIVE—A: *Let's read the first sentence. "Pedro purchased 5 shirts and 3 pairs of pants at the department store." What's the problem with this sentence? Too much information! Remember, when there's more than 1 number in a sentence, we sometimes need to stop after the first number and manipulate the drawing before continuing. Let's try it again: "Pedro·purchased 5 shirts . . ." Based on the drawing, we see only 1 shirt. What do we need to do to the drawing to depict 5 shirts? Great! We'll add 4 more unit bars to Pedro's shirts.*

B: *Now let's continue reading: " . . . and 3 pairs of pants at the department store." How should we adjust our drawing to show Pedro's 3 pairs of pants? Absolutely! We'll add 2 more unit bars for the pants. Now we have 5 units for shirts and 3 units for pants.*

C: *Let's read the next sentence, up to the comma: "All the shirts were the same price, . . ." Does this give us any new information to add to our unit bars? No, so let's move on.*

D

"... and each pair of pants cost $1.20 more than each shirt."

Pedro's shirts

Pedro's pants

+$1.20   +$1.20   +$1.20

HOLD THIS THOUGHT

☛ To show the additional $1.20 for each pair of pants, add "+$1.20" below each "pants" unit in the drawing.

E

"If Pedro spent $163.60 on all of the shirts and pants, ..."

Pedro's shirts

Pedro's pants

+$1.20   +$1.20   +$1.20

} $163.60

E: Let's continue, again reading up to the comma: "If Pedro spent $163.60 on all of the shirts and pants, ..." This talks about the total cost of all of the pants and shirts. The total is $163.60. Where do we put this total value? Yes, let's put it on the right with a brace.

F

"... how much did each shirt cost?"

F: And now let's read the final part of that sentence: "... how much did each shirt cost?" We now need to find the value of 1 shirt.

STEP SIX: *Put the question mark in place.*

Pedro's shirts
?				

$163.60

Pedro's pants

+$1.20   +$1.20   +$1.20

STEP SIX: Since we want the cost of only 1 shirt, we can put a single question mark in 1 of the units for the shirts.

STEP SEVEN: *Work computation to the side or underneath.*

Pedro's shirts	?	$20	$20	$20	$20

Pedro's pants	$20	$20	$20

+$1.20 +$1.20 +$1.20

} $163.60

$1.20 + $1.20 + $1.20 = $3.60
$163.60 − $3.60 = $160

8 units = $160
$160 ÷ 8 = $20
1 unit = $20

STEP EIGHT: *Answer the question in a complete sentence.*

Each of Pedro's shirts cost $20.

STEP SEVEN: *How can we find our answer? What do we need to do first? Why? That's right! First add all of the $1.20s. Since we have 3, what does that total? $3.60? Yes! Can we then take $163.60 and subtract $3.60 to get $160? Absolutely!*

Now we know that 8 units are worth how much? $160. So can we divide the $160 by the number of clothing items (8) to get a total of $20 for each unit? You bet!

STEP EIGHT: *Are we finished with the problem yet? No! What do we still need to do? How would you answer the question in a complete sentence? "Each of Pedro's shirts cost $20."*

MILKING THE PROBLEM FOR ALL IT'S WORTH

▷ **How much did each pair of pants cost?**

▷ **What was the cost of all of the shirts?**

▷ **What was the cost of all of the pants?**

▷ **How much more did Pedro pay for all of the shirts than for all of the pants?**

MULTIPLICATION WITH DECIMALS

Jerry plays computer games an average of 2.5 hours each day. Approximately how many hours does he spend in one year playing computer games?

STEP ONE: *Read the entire problem.*

"Jerry plays computer games an average of 2.5 hours each day. Approximately how many hours does he spend in one year playing computer games?"

STEP TWO: *Decide who is involved in the problem.*

Jerry

STEP THREE: *Decide what is involved in the problem.*

Jerry's
computer
hours

STEP FOUR: *Draw unit bars of equal length.*

Jerry's
computer
hours

STEP FIVE: *Read each sentence, one at a time.*

A

"Jerry plays computer games an average of 2.5 hours each day."

Jerry's
computer
hours

2.5

day

"Teacher Talk"

STEP ONE: *Let's read the entire problem to get an idea of what it's about.*

STEP TWO: *Who are we talking about in this problem? Correct. We're talking about Jerry. Let's write his name below the problem on the left.*

STEP THREE: *What is this problem about? Jerry's what? Are we talking about Jerry's computer games? It says "computer games" in the problem. But let's go to the question. What is it asking us to figure out? How many hours he spends? Great. How can we word this? Let's write "Jerry's computer hours" to show what it is we're trying to figure out.*

STEP FOUR: *Now we need to draw a unit bar that represents Jerry's computer hours.*

STEP FIVE—A: *Let's begin illustrating our problem. Look at the first sentence: "Jerry plays computer games an average of 2.5 hours each day." How might we illustrate this on our unit bar? Let's mark off a segment at the beginning of our unit bar. Let's write "2.5" in that segment and label it "day."*

B

"Approximately how many hours does he spend in one year playing computer games?"

STEP SIX: *Put the question mark in place.*

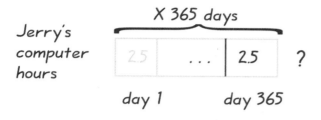

B: *If we continue, we come to the question: "Approximately how many hours does he spend in 1 year playing computer games?" That brings us to the next step.*

STEP SIX: *What is the question? Great! If we examine our unit bar, do we have enough information to place the question mark? You're right: we do not. The question itself provides us with important information, doesn't it? What new information are we given that will help us solve this problem? You're correct: it asks us how many hours in 1 year he spends playing games.*

Let's review up to this point. How many hours, on average, does Jerry play each day? Yes! He plays for 2.5 hours. If we want to know how many hours he plays games in a year, what do you think we need to do? Right! Take the 2.5 hours he plays on average every day and see how many hours that would be in 1 year.

What do we need to know to continue? Absolutely: how many days are in a year? 365! Great! Now, I want to teach you something new.

Our unit bar already shows 2.5 hours with the label of "day." Now that we have more information, let's complete the illustration of our unit bar. How many days are we talking about in this problem? Right. We're talking about 365. We need to show 365 groups of 2.5 hours. Does this create a problem? It would take a tremendous amount of time and space to show 365 groups of 2.5 hours, wouldn't it?

Let me show you how we can use model drawing when we multiply with large numbers. Let's go to our label and instead of simply writing "day," let's write "day 1." Okay? Now, let's go to the end of the unit bar and create a segment that is the same size as the first one in the unit bar. We'll write "2.5" in that segment. Directly below that segment, we'll write the label "day 365." And what should we do with that big segment that's left in the middle? Let's put 3 dots in there.

Does anybody know what those 3 dots are called? That's right: they're an ellipsis. And what do those 3 dots show us? Right again: they show that something's left out. We'll use an ellipsis to represent all the other days between day 1 and day 365. Now, watch this. Directly above the unit bar, we'll draw a brace and write "X 365 days." Does this model now illustrate what we are trying to solve? It's different from problems we've done in the past, but does it show the information and how we need to use it to solve the problem?

Now, where do we put the question mark? Great! We'll put it to the right of the unit bar. The question mark shows what we're trying to find, which in this case is the total.

HOLD THESE THOUGHTS

☞ When multiplying very large numbers, use dots or an ellipsis in the unit bar to represent numbers that are repeated.

☞ The dots/ellipsis approach is used only after students thoroughly understand the model-drawing process.

STEP SEVEN: *Work computation to the side or underneath.*

Jerry's computer hours

X 365 days

| 2.5 | . . . | 2.5 | ? |

day 1   day 365

$365 \times 2.5 \text{ hrs.} = 912.5 \text{ hrs.}$

STEP EIGHT: *Answer the question in a complete sentence.*

Jerry spends approximately 912.5 hours playing computer games in 1 year.

STEP SEVEN: *How should we solve this problem? Sure, we could add 2.5 hours 365 times, but that would take way too much time. Of course, we are going to multiply 365 times 2.5 hours. Let's show this computation below the problem. What's the answer? Is it 912.5 hours? How did you get it? 365 X 2.5 = 912.5? Did anybody do it a different way? Great!*

STEP EIGHT: *How are we going to answer this question? "Jerry spends approximately 912.5 hours playing computer games in 1 year."*

MILKING THE PROBLEM FOR ALL IT'S WORTH

⟫ **What does "approximately" mean?**

⟫ **If Jerry cut the amount of time he spent on computer games each day to 1.7 hours, how many total hours would he spend playing computer games in one year?**

PERCENT

In a class of 30 students, 60% are girls. Find the number of boys in the class.

....

"Teacher Talk"

STEP ONE: Read the entire problem.

"In a class of 30 students, 60% are girls. Find the number of boys in the class."

STEP ONE: *Let's read the entire problem to get an idea of what is happening.*

STEP TWO: Decide who is involved in the problem.

girls

boys

STEP TWO: *Who is involved in this problem? Is Carol? Ty? We do not have individual names of people in this problem, do we? So who are we talking about? That's right: we're talking about "students." But does it tell us specifically what type of students? That's correct: girls and boys. We have 2 variables. Let's list these 2 variables on the left, in the order they appear in the problem.*

STEP THREE: Decide what is involved in the problem.

STEP THREE: *Now, what are we talking about in this problem? Does anything belong to the girls and boys? No. There is no "what" in this problem, so we'll move on to Step Four.*

STEP FOUR: Draw unit bars of equal length.

girls ☐

boys ☐

STEP FOUR: *How many variables do we have? We have 2, so let's draw unit bars of equal length next to the 2 variables.*

STEP FIVE: Read each sentence, one at a time.

A

"In a class of 30 students, . . ."

girls ☐

boys ☐ } 30

STEP FIVE—A: *We're ready to begin solving the problem. Let's read the first sentence. Does everyone see the comma in this sentence? What do we do when we come to a comma? You're right: we stop and illustrate the information in our drawing. "In a class of 30 students, . . ." Stop at the comma! What does the 30 stand for? That's correct: it's the total number of girls and boys. So let's put a brace to the right of both unit bars and write the total of 30. We'll write it way to the side to give ourselves plenty of room.*

B

" . . . 60% are girls."

| | 10% | 20% | 30% | 40% | 50% | 60% |

girls

| | 70% | 80% | 90% | 100% |

boys

} 30

B: *Are we finished with this sentence? No. What does the rest of the sentence say? It says 60% of the students are girls. When we think of percentages, what else do we think of? Decimals and fractions! Great! So if 30 students represent 100%, how many unit bars do we need to show that 60% are girls? Great again! 60% is the same as 6 tenths. Six out of 10 units represent the girls in the class. If we add 5 more unit bars to the first and make sure all of them are the same size, we can show that 60% of the students are girls.*

Let me show you what we do in model drawing when we have problems that involve percents. We can add a "percent ruler" above the bars, like this. When we're dealing with percents, a percent ruler helps to make things clearer. Let's put part of our percent ruler over the girls' units, showing the percentages. Now let's go to the boys' unit bars. How many more equal units do we need to add to their bars? Great. We need to add 3 more units to make a total of 40%, and we need to continue our percent ruler over those units. Now our unit bars represent 100% of the students.

C

"Find the number of boys in the class."

C: *Let's move to the next sentence: "Find the number of boys in the class." Do you see that this is really our question? So here we go to the next step.*

STEP SIX: *Put the question mark in place.*

STEP SIX: *We need to put the question mark in place in our drawing. Where's the question mark in our problem? There isn't one, is there? Does that mean we don't have a question to answer? No, it means the question is* implied, *and we have to figure out what's being asked. So what are we being asked here? How many boys are in the class? That's right! Let's look at the unit bars. Where should we write the question mark? Yes, let's put it to the right of the boys' unit bars because that shows the total number of boys, which is what we are asked to solve.*

HOLD THESE THOUGHTS

☞ When dealing with percents, a percent ruler helps to make things clearer.

☞ Sometimes a problem doesn't include a question mark. The question is implied. The implied question tells you where to place the question mark in the drawing.

STEP SEVEN: *Work computation to the side or underneath.*

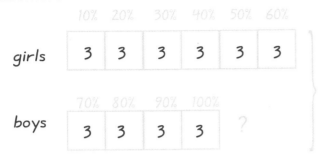

	10%	20%	30%	40%	50%	60%
girls	3	3	3	3	3	3

	70%	80%	90%	100%		
boys	3	3	3	3	?	

30

10 units = 30
30 ÷ 10 = 3
1 unit = 3
4 X 3 = 12

STEP EIGHT: *Answer the question in a complete sentence.*

There are 12 boys in the class.

STEP SEVEN: *Do we have all the information we need to solve this problem? Yes, we do. How should we solve it? What do we need to do first? Good: we need to figure out the value of each tenth. If 10 units equal 30, and 30 divided by 10 is 3, then 1 unit equals 3. Let's show this division below the problem. Let's label each tenth with a value of "3."*

What is the next step? Great! We take 4 groups of boys times 3 to get a total of 12 boys.

STEP EIGHT: *How should we answer this question? Can we borrow some words from the question to write the answer? Great! "There are 12 boys in the class."*

MILKING THE PROBLEM FOR ALL IT'S WORTH

▸ How many girls are in the class?

▸ How many more girls than boys are in the class?

▸ What is the ratio of girls to boys in the class?

PERCENT

An auditorium seats 1,500 students. Of all those seats, 70% are in the orchestra section and the rest are in the balcony. How many more seats are in the orchestra section than in the balcony?

....

STEP ONE: *Read the entire problem.*

"An auditorium seats 1,500 students. Of all those seats, 70% are in the orchestra section and the rest are in the balcony. How many more seats are in the orchestra section than in the balcony?"

STEP TWO: *Decide who is involved in the problem.*

students

STEP THREE: *Decide what is involved in the problem.*

students'
seats

STEP FOUR: *Draw unit bars of equal length.*

students'
seats

STEP FIVE: *Read each sentence, one at a time.*

A

"An auditorium seats 1,500 students."

students'
seats   *1,500*

" Teacher Talk "

STEP ONE: *Let's read the problem.*

STEP TWO: *Who is involved? Is there a specific person or group of people involved in this problem? "Students" is correct. How many variables does that account for? Yes, 1 variable.*

STEP THREE: *What is involved in the problem? The students' what? "Students' seats" is what we're looking for, so that's what we should write. Sometimes in the past we've broken problems like this into 2 variables, but this time I'd like to show you another way we can solve it.*

STEP FOUR: *How many variables do we have now? Still just 1? Great! So how many unit bars do we need? And with 1 bar, how large should it be? That's right: 1 large bar is what we need.*

STEP FIVE—A: *Let's read the first sentence: "An auditorium seats 1,500 students." Where are we going to put the 1,500? Yes, let's put it at the end of the bar, to the right.*

B

"Of all those seats, 70% are in the orchestra section . . ."

	10%	20%	30%	40%	50%	60%	70%	80%	90%	100%
students' seats	O	O	O	O	O	O	O			

1,500

B: *Let's read on. What's the problem with the second sentence? Too much information! So let's deal with part of this sentence at a time, starting with the beginning: "Of all those seats, 70% are in the orchestra section . . ."*

When we're working with percents, the whole bar equals 100%. How are we going to show 70% within that large bar of 100%? Great! Divide the bar into 10 units. Then what should we add? Yes! We're going to add a percent ruler above the bar and label the segments from 10% to 100%. Then we're going to go inside the bar and label 7 of the units "O" for "orchestra." Now let's finish the sentence.

C

". . . and the rest are in the balcony."

	10%	20%	30%	40%	50%	60%	70%	80%	90%	100%
students' seats	O	O	O	O	O	O	O	B	B	B

1,500

C: *We see that the rest are in the balcony. So we'll label the rest of the bars with what letter? Why "B"? For "balcony." Great!*

D

"How many more seats are in the orchestra section than in the balcony?"

D: *Now comes the question: "How many more seats are in the orchestra section than in the balcony?"*

HOLD THIS THOUGHT

☞ Percent rulers don't always have to be in increments of 10 percent. They do need to be in increments that easily divide into 100. Use 20-percent increments or 50-percent increments when that's more appropriate.

STEP SIX: *Put the question mark in place.*

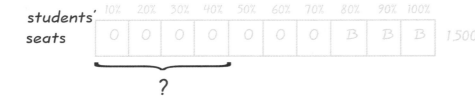

students' seats | 10% 20% 30% 40% 50% 60% 70% 80% 90% 100%

| O | O | O | O | O | O | O | B | B | B | 1,500

?

STEP SEVEN: *Work computation to the side or underneath.*

students' seats | 10% 20% 30% 40% 50% 60% 70% 80% 90% 100%

| O | O | O | O | O | O | O | B | B | B | 1,500
| 150 | 150 | 150 | 150 | 150 | 150 | 150 | 150 | 150 | 150 |

?

10 units = 1,500
1500 ÷ 10 = 150
1 unit = 150

150 X 4 = 600
OR
(100 X 4) + (50 X 4) = 600
OR
150 + 150 + 150 + 150 = 600
OR
150 + 150 = 300
300 + 300 = 600

STEP EIGHT: *Answer the question in a complete sentence.*

There are 600 more seats in the orchestra section than in the balcony of the auditorium.

STEP SIX: *We have 7 units for the orchestra and 3 units for the balcony. We can put our question mark under 4 of the orchestra units because there are 4 more units of orchestra than balcony.*

STEP SEVEN: *If the entire bar is worth 1,500, then 10 units are worth 1,500. How can we find out what each unit is worth? Great! Divide 1,500 by 10 to find each unit, or each 10%. How much is each unit worth? That's right: each unit is worth 150. Now what do we do next? Take 150 and multiply it by 4? Sure. How else could you find the answer? Fantastic! Take 100 and multiply it by 4, take 50 and multiply it by 4, and then add the answers together.*

Other ideas? Yes, you could add 150 four times.

Anybody else? Great! Double 150 and then double that result.

In all cases, the answer is 600.

STEP EIGHT: *How would you answer the question in a complete sentence? "There are 600 more seats in the orchestra section than in the balcony of the auditorium."*

MILKING THE PROBLEM FOR ALL IT'S WORTH

▸ **How many seats are in the balcony?**

▸ **How many seats are in the orchestra section?**

ALGEBRA

Juan and Nigel have $25 between them. If Juan has $7 more than Nigel, how much money does Nigel have?

"Teacher Talk"

STEP ONE: *Read the entire problem.*

"Juan and Nigel have $25 between them. If Juan has $7 more than Nigel, how much money does Nigel have?"

STEP ONE: *Let's read the entire problem to picture what we're being asked to solve.*

STEP TWO: *Decide who is involved in the problem.*

Juan

Nigel

STEP TWO: *Who is involved in this problem? Juan and Nigel are involved. Great! Let's list their names vertically below the problem on the left side of the paper.*

STEP THREE: *Decide what is involved in the problem.*

Juan's money

Nigel's money

STEP THREE: *Now that we know Juan and Nigel are involved in the problem, we can ask, "Juan's and Nigel's what?" What is involved in this problem? Are we talking about their shoes? Their lunch? No, we're talking about their money. You're correct. We want to write "money" below both Juan's and Nigel's names so we see "Juan's money" and "Nigel's money."*

STEP FOUR: *Draw unit bars of equal length.*

Juan's money	

Nigel's money	

STEP FOUR: *Since we have determined that 2 variables are present in this problem, we need to draw 2 unit bars of equal length— 1 next to Juan's name and 1 next to Nigel's name.*

STEP FIVE: *Read each sentence, one at a time.*

A

"Juan and Nigel have $25 between them."

B

"If Juan has $7 more than Nigel, . . ."

C

" . . . how much money does Nigel have?"

STEP SIX: *Put the question mark in place.*

STEP FIVE—A: *Now we're ready to begin solving the problem. Let's read the first sentence. "Juan and Nigel have $25 between them." Do they* each *have $25? No, they share a total of $25. We show this by drawing a brace to the right of both Juan's and Nigel's unit bars and writing the total of "$25." This now shows that they have $25 between them.*

B: *Let's go on to the next sentence. Read to the comma, and then let's stop and record the information we've learned. "If Juan has $7 more than Nigel, . . ." Let's go to the unit bars. Who has more money? Juan? How much more? That's right: $7. Right now their unit bars look like they have exactly the same amount of money. Do they? No, Juan has more. How much more again? $7. What do we need to do to Juan's unit bar? Great! We need to add to it and write "$7" in the added part. Now can we look at the unit bars and see that Juan has $7 more than Nigel? Great!*

Do we know how much money Nigel has? No, not yet? How about Juan? No, we know only that he has $7 more than Nigel.

C: *Let's continue after the comma: ". . . how much money does Nigel have?" This is the question we need to answer, so let's move on to the next step.*

STEP SIX: *What is the question we are answering? Are we looking for Juan's money? No. Are we looking for Nigel's money? Yes, we are. Where should we put the question mark to show we are looking for Nigel's total money? Yes, let's put it in his unit bar.*

STEP SEVEN: *Work computation to the side or underneath.*

| Juan's money | | $9 | | $7 | |
| Nigel's money | | ? | |

$25

$25 - $7 = $18
2 units = $18
$18 ÷ 2 = $9
1 unit = $9

STEP EIGHT: *Answer the question in a complete sentence.*

Nigel has $9.

HOLD THIS THOUGHT

☛ Once you get an answer, go back and check. Is the answer reasonable?

STEP SEVEN: *Let's solve the problem. What do we know? We know that the 2 boys share a total of $25 and that Juan has $7 more than Nigel. What's our first step? Correct. We need to subtract the $7 we know that Juan has from the total of $25. Let's do the computation below the problem. The difference is $18.*

Now what can you tell me about the $18? Who can explain what this amount represents? Great! It represents the money left that the 2 boys share. So 2 units are worth how much? $18? Fantastic! Now, how can we compute how much money each boy has? That's right. Let's divide $18 by 2, working below the drawing. What is the answer? $9. So 1 unit equals $9. Where will we write "$9"? Yes, we'll write it in the first part of Juan's unit bar.

Let's check our computation. $9 + $9 + $7 = $25. Our answer is reasonable!

By looking at Nigel's unit bar, can we tell how much money he has? Yes, $9 is correct.

STEP EIGHT: *How can we answer this question in a complete sentence? "Nigel has $9."*

MILKING THE PROBLEM FOR ALL IT'S WORTH

⇒ **How much money does Juan have?**

⇒ **What fraction of the total is Nigel's money?**

⇒ **What fraction of the total is Juan's money?**

PROBLEMS FOR INDEPENDENT PRACTICE

ADDITION

Nicole had 3 stuffed animals in her toy chest. She had 5 stuffed animals on her bed. How many stuffed animals did she have altogether?

ADDITION

It snowed for 3 days in a row in December. It snowed 6 inches on Tuesday, 8 on Wednesday, and 6 on Thursday. How many total inches of snow fell during the 3 days?

ADDITION

Nicole had 3 stuffed animals in her toy chest. She had 5 stuffed animals on her bed. How many stuffed animals did she have altogether?

Nicole's stuffed animals in toy chest

| 1 | 1 | 1 | 3

Nicole's stuffed animals on bed

| 1 | 1 | 1 | 1 | 1 | 5

? 3 + 5 = 8

Nicole had 8 stuffed animals altogether.

ADDITION

It snowed for 3 days in a row in December. It snowed 6 inches on Tuesday, 8 on Wednesday, and 6 on Thursday. How many total inches of snow fell during the 3 days?

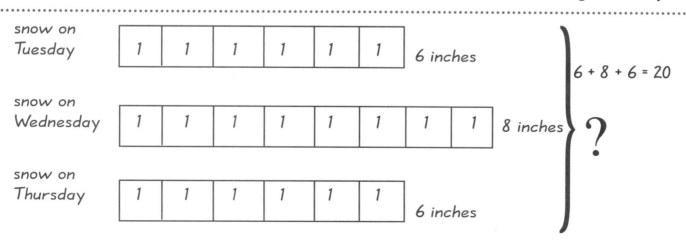

snow on Tuesday

| 1 | 1 | 1 | 1 | 1 | 1 | 6 inches

snow on Wednesday

| 1 | 1 | 1 | 1 | 1 | 1 | 1 | 1 | 8 inches

snow on Thursday

| 1 | 1 | 1 | 1 | 1 | 1 | 6 inches

6 + 8 + 6 = 20 ?

A total of 20 inches of snow fell during the 3 days.

ADDITION

Jolina bought 9 pens, 3 pencils, 3 erasers, and a calculator for school. How many items did she purchase?

ADDITION

There were 3 second-grade classrooms at Dublin Elementary School. There were 21 students in the first class, 23 in the second, and 22 in the third. How many second-grade students were there at Dublin Elementary School?

ADDITION

Jolina bought 9 pens, 3 pencils, 3 erasers, and a calculator for school. How many items did she purchase?

Jolina's pens

| 1 | 1 | 1 | 1 | 1 | 1 | 1 | 1 | 1 | 9

Jolina's pencils

| 1 | 1 | 1 | 3

Jolina's erasers

| 1 | 1 | 1 | 3

Jolina's calculator

| 1 | 1

}

?

$9 + 3 + 3 + 1 = 16$

Jolina purchased 16 items for school.

ADDITION

There were 3 second-grade classrooms at Dublin Elementary School. There were 21 students in the first class, 23 in the second, and 22 in the third. How many second-grade students were there at Dublin Elementary School?

second-grade students in first class | 21

second-grade students in second class | 23

second-grade students in third class | 22

}

?

$21 + 23 + 22 = 66$

There were 66 second-grade students at Dublin Elementary School.

ADDITION

Three friends saved money over the summer. Kim saved $545, Caitlin saved $630, and Erin saved $35 more than Caitlin. What is the total amount of money saved by the 3 friends?

....

SUBTRACTION

A pet store had 9 dogs. The store sold 3 of the dogs. How many dogs were left in the pet store?

....

ADDITION

Three friends saved money over the summer. Kim saved $545, Caitlin saved $630, and Erin saved $35 more than Caitlin. What is the total amount of money saved by the 3 friends?

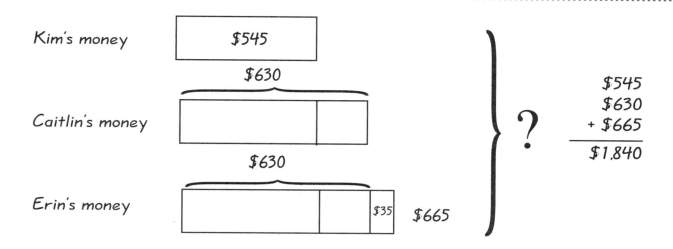

Kim's money — $545

Caitlin's money — $630

Erin's money — $630 | $35 | $665

$$\begin{array}{r} \$545 \\ \$630 \\ + \ \$665 \\ \hline \$1,840 \end{array}$$

?

Kim, Caitlin, and Erin saved a total of $1,840 over the summer.

SUBTRACTION

A pet store had 9 dogs. The store sold 3 of the dogs. How many dogs were left in the pet store?

dogs | ? L | S / 3 | 9

$9 - 3 = 6$

There were 6 dogs left in the pet store.

SUBTRACTION

Maria had a collection of 56 stamps from around the world. If she gave away 14 stamps, how many did she have left in her collection?

SUBTRACTION

Liza earned $500 as her weekly pay. She paid $413 to cover her bills for the week. How much money did she have left to spend?

SUBTRACTION

Maria had a collection of 56 stamps from around the world. If she gave away 14 stamps, how many did she have left in her collection?

Maria's
stamps

$56 - 14 = 42$

Maria had 42 stamps left in her collection.

SUBTRACTION

Liza earned $500 as her weekly pay. She paid $413 to cover her bills for the week. How much money did she have left to spend?

Liza's
money

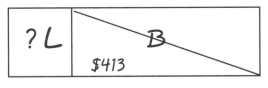

$500 - $413 = $87

Liza had $87 left to spend.

SUBTRACTION

A movie theater has 1,250 seats. If 756 people attend today's matinee, how many empty seats will there be in the movie theater?

SUBTRACTION

The trip from Amber City to Pineville is 756 miles. Sandra drove 336 miles on Monday and 249 miles on Tuesday. How many more miles must Sandra drive on Wednesday to complete the trip?

SUBTRACTION

A movie theater has 1,250 seats. If 756 people attend today's matinee, how many empty seats will there be in the movie theater?

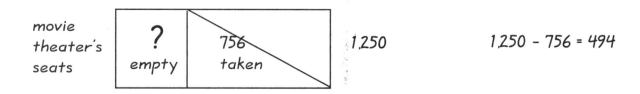

1,250   1,250 − 756 = 494

There will be 494 empty seats in the movie theater.

SUBTRACTION

The trip from Amber City to Pineville is 756 miles. Sandra drove 336 miles on Monday and 249 miles on Tuesday. How many more miles must Sandra drive on Wednesday to complete the trip?

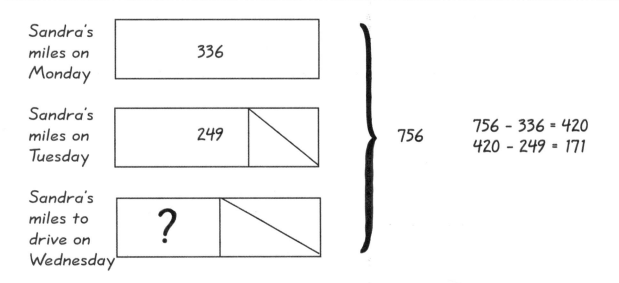

756   756 − 336 = 420
             420 − 249 = 171

Sandra must drive 171 more miles on Wednesday to complete the trip.

MIXED OPERATIONS (+ & −)

Sue had 25 fewer coins than Anne Marie. If Anne Marie had 45 coins, how many coins did Sue and Anne Marie have altogether?

....

MIXED OPERATIONS (+ & −)

The bakers made 1,000 cookies for the party. They made 345 ginger cookies and 320 chocolate chip cookies. The rest were oatmeal raisin. How many oatmeal raisin cookies did the bakers make for the party?

....

MIXED OPERATIONS (+ & –)

Sue had 25 fewer coins than Anne Marie. If Anne Marie had 45 coins, how many coins did Sue and Anne Marie have altogether?

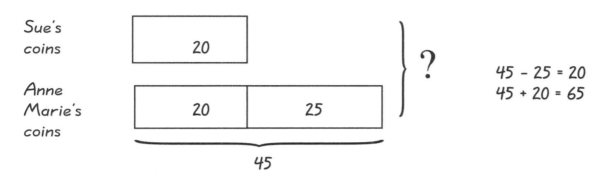

45 – 25 = 20
45 + 20 = 65

Sue and Anne Marie had 65 coins altogether.

MIXED OPERATIONS (+ & –)

The bakers made 1,000 cookies for the party. They made 345 ginger cookies and 320 chocolate chip cookies. The rest were oatmeal raisin. How many oatmeal raisin cookies did the bakers make for the party?

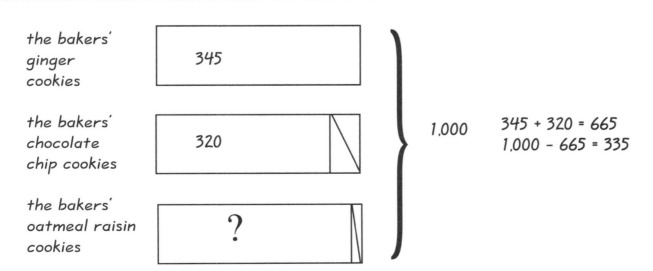

345 + 320 = 665
1,000 – 665 = 335

The bakers made 335 oatmeal raisin cookies for the party.

MULTIPLICATION

There are 6 bags of cookies on the store counter. If each bag has 8 cookies, how many cookies are there in all?

MULTIPLICATION

Katrina ran 3 miles last weekend. Tyrone ran 4 times as many miles as Katrina. How many miles did Tyrone run last weekend?

MULTIPLICATION

There are 6 bags of cookies on the store counter. If each bag has 8 cookies, how many cookies are there in all?

bags of cookies

| C 8 | C 8 | C 8 | C 8 | C 8 | C 8 | ?

$6 \times 8 = 48$

There are 48 cookies in all.

MULTIPLICATION

Katrina ran 3 miles last weekend. Tyrone ran 4 times as many miles as Katrina. How many miles did Tyrone run last weekend?

Katrina's miles

| 3 |

Tyrone's miles

| 3 | 3 | 3 | 3 | ?

$4 \times 3 = 12$

Tyrone ran 12 miles last weekend.

MULTIPLICATION

The students at a local elementary school collected aluminum cans for a fundraising activity. At the end of the first week, they had 10 boxes with 30 cans in each box. How many cans did they collect the first week of the fundraiser?
....

MULTIPLICATION

Cynthia had 4 trays of egg rolls to bring to the party. Each tray had 45 egg rolls. How many egg rolls did she bring to the party?
....

MULTIPLICATION

The students at a local elementary school collected aluminum cans for a fundraising activity. At the end of the first week, they had 10 boxes with 30 cans in each box. How many cans did they collect the first week of the fundraiser?

boxes of aluminum cans

30	30	30	30	30	30	30	30	30	30

?   10 X 30 = 300

The students collected 300 cans during the first week of the fundraiser.

MULTIPLICATION

Cynthia had 4 trays of egg rolls to bring to the party. Each tray had 45 egg rolls. How many egg rolls did she bring to the party?

Cynthia's trays of egg rolls

45	45	45	45

?   4 X 45 = 180

Cynthia brought 180 egg rolls to the party.

MULTIPLICATION

Cheryl and Joe were collecting money for a charitable event. Cheryl collected 4 times as much money as Joe collected. If Joe collected $150, how much did they collect together?

MULTIPLICATION

A concert hall holds 1,362 people. During the month of May, the orchestra performed every evening, and every performance was sold out. How many tickets were sold during the month of May?

MULTIPLICATION

Cheryl and Joe were collecting money for a charitable event. Cheryl collected 4 times as much money as Joe collected. If Joe collected $150, how much did they collect together?

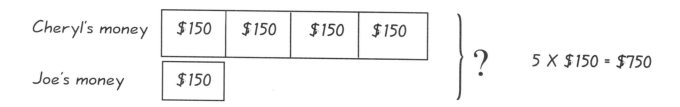

| Cheryl's money | $150 | $150 | $150 | $150 |

| Joe's money | $150 |

} ?

5 X $150 = $750

Together, Cheryl and Joe collected $750 for the charitable event.

MULTIPLICATION

A concert hall holds 1,362 people. During the month of May, the orchestra performed every evening, and every performance was sold out. How many tickets were sold during the month of May?

X 31 days

concert hall tickets during May

| 1,362 | ... | 1,362 |

May 1   May 31

?

31 X 1,362 = 42,222

During the month of May, 42,222 tickets were sold.

MIXED OPERATIONS (X & ÷)

Bill had twice as many toy cars as Rich and 4 times as many as Colin. If Rich had 18 toy cars in his collection, how many did the 3 boys have altogether?

....

MIXED OPERATIONS (X & +)

Mandy had 4 packages of chocolate candy with 6 pieces in each package. She bought 2 packages of peanut butter candy with 3 pieces in each package. How many pieces of candy did Mandy have in all?

....

MIXED OPERATIONS (X & ÷)

Bill had twice as many toy cars as Rich and 4 times as many as Colin. If Rich had 18 toy cars in his collection, how many did the 3 boys have altogether?

Bill's
toy cars

9	9	9	9

Rich's
toy cars

9	9

Colin's
toy cars

9

}?

2 units = 18
18 ÷ 2 = 9
1 unit = 9
7 X 9 = 63

Bill, Rich, and Colin had 63 toy cars altogether.

MIXED OPERATIONS (X & +)

Mandy had 4 packages of chocolate candy with 6 pieces in each package. She bought 2 packages of peanut butter candy with 3 pieces in each package. How many pieces of candy did Mandy have in all?

Mandy's
packages of
chocolate candy

6	6	6	6
24

Mandy's
packages of
peanut butter
candy

3	3
6

}?

4 X 6 = 24
2 X 3 = 6
24 + 6 = 30

Mandy had 30 pieces of candy in all.

DIVISION

The teacher divided 20 students into 4 equal groups. How many students were in each group?

....

DIVISION

Josh is in charge of lining up the band for the parade. If there are 24 band members and he wants to put them into 6 equal rows, how many band members will be in each row?

....

DIVISION

The teacher divided 20 students into 4 equal groups. How many students were in each group?

students | ? | | | | 20

4 units = 20
20 ÷ 4 = 5
1 unit = 5

There were 5 students in each group.

DIVISION

Josh is in charge of lining up the band for the parade. If there are 24 band members and he wants to put them into 6 equal rows, how many band members will be in each row?

band members | ? | | | | | | 24

6 units = 24
24 ÷ 6 = 4
1 unit = 4

There will be 4 band members in each row.

DIVISION

Lola is putting her books on shelves in the bookcase. She has 736 books to put on 4 shelves. If she puts an equal number of books on each shelf, how many books will she put on each shelf?

DIVISION WITH DECIMALS

Jasmine made 32 ounces of shampoo in her science class. She poured the shampoo into 5 bottles. If she divided the shampoo evenly, approximately how much shampoo did she pour into each bottle?

DIVISION

Lola is putting her books on shelves in the bookcase. She has 736 books to put on 4 shelves. If she puts an equal number of books on each shelf, how many books will she put on each shelf?

| Lola's books | ? | 184 | 184 | 184 | 736

4 units = 736

736 ÷ 4 = 184

1 unit = 184

Lola will put 184 books on each shelf.

DIVISION WITH DECIMALS

Jasmine made 32 ounces of shampoo in her science class. She poured the shampoo into 5 bottles. If she divided the shampoo evenly, approximately how much shampoo did she pour into each bottle?

5 units = 32 oz.

| Jasmine's shampoo (in ounces) | ? | 6.4 | 6.4 | 6.4 | 6.4 | 32

$$5)\overline{32.0} = 6.4$$

1 unit = 6.4 oz.

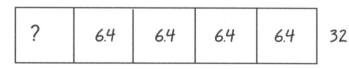

Jasmine poured approximately 6.4 ounces of shampoo into each bottle.

MIXED OPERATIONS (– & ÷)

Kevin and Joaquim had a total of $620. Joaquim had $100 more than Kevin. How much money did Kevin have?

....

DIVISION

Becca bought a 12-page photo album. If she has a total of 49 photographs, how many should she put on each page?

....

MIXED OPERATIONS (– & ÷)

Kevin and Joaquim had a total of $620. Joaquim had $100 more than Kevin. How much money did Kevin have?

Kevin's money

?

Joaquim's money

$260	$100

} $620

$620 – $100 = $520
2 units = $520

$$2 \overline{)520} = 260$$

1 unit = $260

Kevin had $260.

DIVISION

Becca bought a 12-page photo album. If she has a total of 49 photos, how many should she put on each page?

Becca's photos

p. 1	p. 2	p. 3	p. 4	p. 5	p. 6	p. 7	p. 8	p. 9	p. 10	p. 11	p. 12	
? 4	4	4	4	4	4	4	4	4	4	4	4	1	49

12 units = 49
49 ÷ 12 = 4 R1
1 unit = 4, with 1 left over

Becca should put 4 photographs on each page, except one page will need to have 5 photos.

DIVISION

At the wedding, 1,000 flowers were arranged on 25 tables. If the flowers were divided evenly, how many flowers were on each table?

MIXED OPERATIONS (÷ & +)

A local garden center ordered 14 shrubs that had a total sales price of $280. In addition to the sales price, there was a $1 handling fee for each shrub. What was the final cost of each shrub, including handling?

DIVISION

At the wedding, 1,000 flowers were arranged on 25 tables. If the flowers were divided evenly, how many flowers were on each table?

1,000

flowers
on
tables

| ? | 40 | 40 | 40 | 40 | 40 | 40 | 40 | 40 | 40 | 40 | 40 | 40 | 40 | 40 | 40 | 40 | 40 | 40 | 40 | 40 | 40 | 40 | 40 | 40 |

25 units = 1,000

$$25\overline{)1{,}000} = 40$$

There were 40 flowers on each table.

1 unit = 40

MIXED OPERATIONS (÷ & +)

A local garden center ordered 14 shrubs that had a total sales price of $280. In addition to the sales price, there was a $1 handling fee for each shrub. What was the final cost of each shrub, including handling?

shrubs'
cost

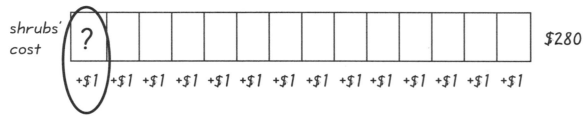

$280

14 units = $280
$280 ÷ 14 = $20
1 unit = $20

The final cost of each shrub, including handling, was $21.

$20 + $1 = $21

DIVISION

Gianna and Laura spent $900 at the gym last year. If Gianna spent half as much as Laura did, how much did Gianna spend at the gym?

···

MIXED OPERATIONS (– & ÷)

Jan and Olivia have $36 altogether. Jan has $14 more than Olivia. How much money does Olivia have?

···

DIVISION

Gianna and Laura spent $900 at the gym last year. If Gianna spent half as much as Laura did, how much did Gianna spend at the gym?

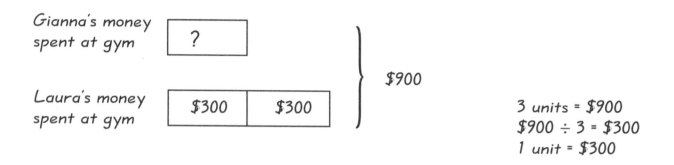

Gianna spent $300 at the gym last year.

MIXED OPERATIONS (− & ÷)

Jan and Olivia have $36 altogether. Jan has $14 more than Olivia. How much money does Olivia have?

Jan's money | $11 | $14
Olivia's money | $11 | ?
} $36

$36 − $14 = $22
2 units = $22
$22 ÷ 2 = $11
1 unit = $11

Olivia has $11.

MIXED OPERATIONS (+, − & ÷)

The total weight of Fatimah, Ginger, and Michelle is 123 pounds. Fatimah is 15 pounds heavier than Ginger. Ginger is 3 pounds lighter than Michelle. Find Michelle's weight.

MIXED OPERATIONS (X & ÷)

Stella has twice as many fish in her tank as Catherine. Catherine has twice as many fish in her tank as Rita. They have 70 fish altogether. How many fish does Rita have in her tank?

MIXED OPERATIONS (+, – & ÷)

The total weight of Fatimah, Ginger, and Michelle is 123 pounds. Fatimah is 15 pounds heavier than Ginger. Ginger is 3 pounds lighter than Michelle. Find Michelle's weight.

Fatimah's weight (in lbs.) | 35 | 15

Ginger's weight (in lbs.) | 35

Michelle's weight (in lbs.) | 35 | 3 | ?

} 123

15 + 3 = 18
123 – 18 = 105
3 units = 105

$$3\overline{)105} = 35$$

1 unit = 35
35 + 3 = 38

Michelle weighs 38 pounds.

MIXED OPERATIONS (X & ÷)

Stella has twice as many fish in her tank as Catherine. Catherine has twice as many fish in her tank as Rita. They have 70 fish altogether. How many fish does Rita have in her tank?

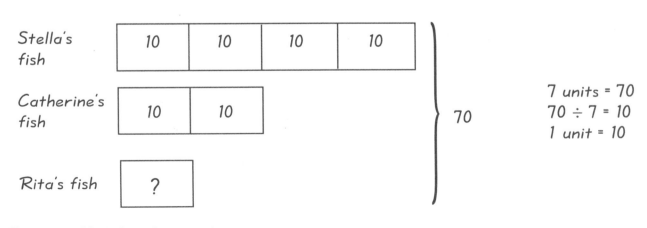

Stella's fish | 10 | 10 | 10 | 10

Catherine's fish | 10 | 10

Rita's fish | ?

} 70

7 units = 70
70 ÷ 7 = 10
1 unit = 10

Rita has 10 fish in her tank.

FRACTIONS

At the party, 3/5 of the girls had brown hair. If 12 girls did *not* have brown hair, how many girls were at the party?

··

FRACTIONS

Grace has 28 marbles. Of the total marbles, 3/7 are red and the rest are blue. How many blue marbles does Grace have?

··

FRACTIONS

At the party, 3/5 of the girls had brown hair. If 12 girls did *not* have brown hair, how many girls were at the party?

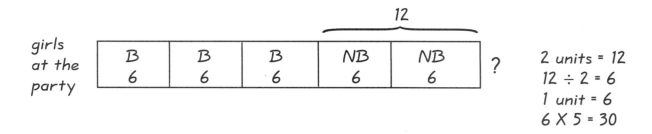

| girls at the party | B 6 | B 6 | B 6 | NB 6 | NB 6 | ? |

2 units = 12
12 ÷ 2 = 6
1 unit = 6
6 X 5 = 30

There were 30 girls at the party.

FRACTIONS

Grace has 28 marbles. Of the total marbles, 3/7 are red and the rest are blue. How many blue marbles does Grace have?

Grace's red marbles | 4 | 4 | 4

Grace's blue marbles | 4 | 4 | 4 | 4 | ?

28

7 units = 28
28 ÷ 7 = 4
1 unit = 4
4 X 4 = 16

Grace has 16 blue marbles.

FRACTIONS

The candy shop made 400 Valentine candies. The shop sold 5/8 of them before Valentine's Day and 1/5 of the remainder on Valentine's Day itself. How many Valentine candies were left after Valentine's Day?

....

FRACTIONS

Evelyn read 25 pages of a book on Friday morning. She read 1/4 of the remainder on Friday afternoon. If she still had 90 pages to read after Friday afternoon, how many pages were in the book?

....

FRACTIONS

The candy shop made 400 Valentine candies. The shop sold 5/8 of them before Valentine's Day and 1/5 of the <u>remainder</u> on Valentine's Day itself. How many Valentine candies were left after Valentine's Day?

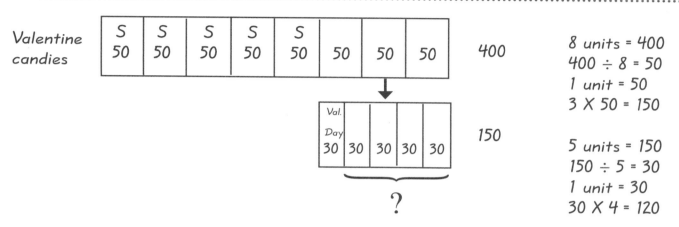

8 units = 400
400 ÷ 8 = 50
1 unit = 50
3 X 50 = 150

5 units = 150
150 ÷ 5 = 30
1 unit = 30
30 X 4 = 120

After Valentine's Day, 120 Valentine candies were left.

FRACTIONS

Evelyn read 25 pages of a book on Friday morning. She read 1/4 of the <u>remainder</u> on Friday afternoon. If she still had 90 pages to read after Friday afternoon, how many pages were in the book?

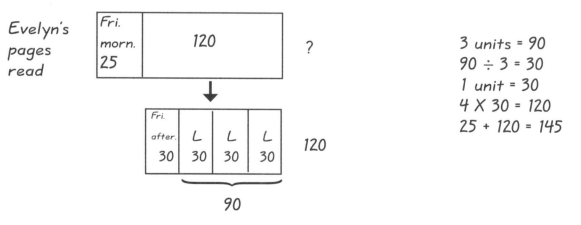

3 units = 90
90 ÷ 3 = 30
1 unit = 30
4 X 30 = 120
25 + 120 = 145

There were 145 pages in the book.

FRACTIONS

Angela earned $150 doing odd jobs over the summer. She put 2/3 of the money in savings. She then spent 1/2 of the remaining money on clothes. How much money does she have left to spend on other things?.

···

RATE

James typed 75 words a minute for 8 minutes. How many words did he type in 8 minutes?

···

FRACTIONS

Angela earned $150 doing odd jobs over the summer. She put 2/3 of the money in savings. She then spent 1/2 of the <u>remaining</u> money on clothes. How much money does she have left to spend on other things?

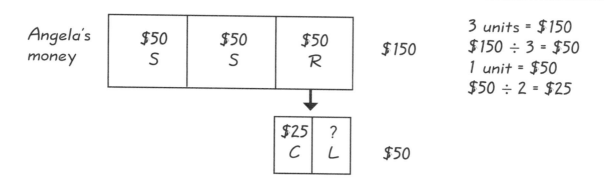

Angela has $25 left to spend on other things.

RATE

James typed 75 words a minute for 8 minutes. How many words did he type in 8 minutes?

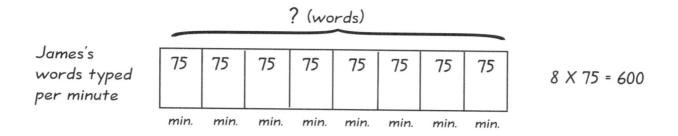

James typed 600 words in 8 minutes.

RATE

Sulin ran 6 miles in 100 minutes. How many minutes did it take her to run 1 mile?

RATIO

In a class of 35 students, the ratio of girls to boys is 3 : 4. How many more boys than girls are there?

RATE

Sulin ran 6 miles in 100 minutes. How many minutes did it take her to run 1 mile?

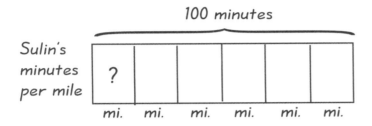

6 units = 100 min.
100 ÷ 6 = 16 min. 40 sec.
1 unit = 16 min. 40 sec.

It took Sulin 16 minutes and 40 seconds to run a mile.

RATIO

In a class of 35 students, the ratio of girls to boys is 3 : 4. How many more boys than girls are there?

girls | 5 | 5 | 5 |

boys | 5 | 5 | 5 | ? |

} 35

7 units = 35
35 ÷ 7 = 5
1 unit = 5

There are 5 more boys than girls in the class.

RATIO

The ratio of male teachers to female teachers in middle schools around the United States is 2 : 7. If there is an average of 49 female teachers in each school, how many male teachers are there, on average, in each school?

....

RATIO

There are 30 dogs, cats, and hamsters altogether at a pet store. The ratio of dogs to cats to hamsters is 5 : 3 : 2. How many dogs and cats are there at the pet store?

....

RATIO

The ratio of male teachers to female teachers in middle schools around the United States is 2 : 7. If there is an average of 49 female teachers in each school, how many male teachers are there, on average, in each school?

male teachers	7	7	?

female teachers	7	7	7	7	7	7	7	49

7 units = 49
49 ÷ 7 = 7
1 unit = 7
2 X 7 = 14

There are 14 male teachers, on average, in each school.

RATIO

There are 30 dogs, cats, and hamsters altogether at a pet store. The ratio of dogs to cats to hamsters is 5 : 3 : 2. How many dogs and cats are there at the pet store?

dogs	3	3	3	3	3	15

cats	3	3	3	9

hamsters	3	3

?

30

10 units = 30
30 ÷ 10 = 3
1 unit = 3

5 X 3 = 15
3 X 3 = 9
15 + 9 = 24

There are 24 dogs and cats at the pet store.

RATIO

A 540-foot-long street in New Orleans was painted purple, yellow, and red for the festival in the ratio 2 : 3 : 5. How many feet of the street were painted yellow?

......

MIXED OPERATIONS (+, – & X WITH DECIMALS)

Fantasia had 32 coins. Of the total coins, 10 were quarters, 8 were dimes, 3 were nickels, and the rest were pennies. What was the value of all of her pennies?

......

RATIO

A 540-foot-long street in New Orleans was painted purple, yellow, and red for the festival in the ratio 2 : 3 : 5. How many feet of the street were painted yellow?

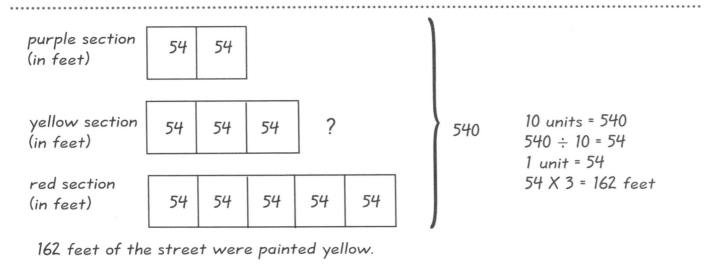

162 feet of the street were painted yellow.

MIXED OPERATIONS (+, – & X WITH DECIMALS)

Fantasia had 32 coins. Of the total coins, 10 were quarters, 8 were dimes, 3 were nickels, and the rest were pennies. What was the value of all of her pennies?

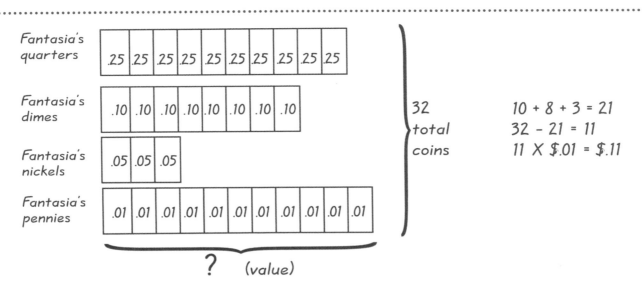

The value of all of Fantasia's pennies was $.11.

ADDITION & MULTIPLICATION WITH DECIMALS

Ramon bought 3 bottles of water for $1.25 each and 3 bottles of soda for $1.50 each. How much money did he spend altogether?

ADDITION OF DECIMALS

Jeff bought a magazine for $3.50, a bottle of soda for $1.25, and a book for $10.25. How much money did he spend?

ADDITION & MULTIPLICATION WITH DECIMALS

Ramon bought 3 bottles of water for $1.25 each and 3 bottles of soda for $1.50 each. How much money did he spend altogether?

3 X $1.25 = $3.75
3 X $1.50 = $4.50
$3.75 + $4.50 = $8.25

Ramon spent $8.25 altogether for water and soda.

ADDITION OF DECIMALS

Jeff bought a magazine for $3.50, a bottle of soda for $1.25, and a book for $10.25. How much money did he spend?

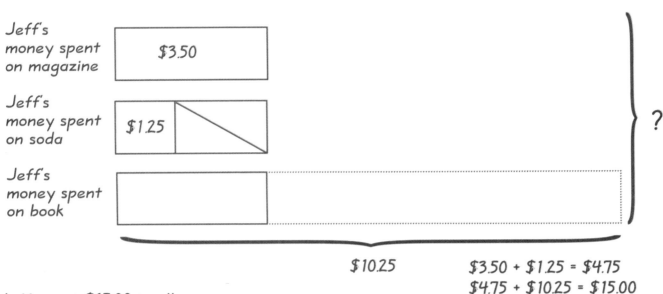

$3.50 + $1.25 = $4.75
$4.75 + $10.25 = $15.00

Jeff spent $15.00 in all.

SUBTRACTION OF DECIMALS

Karen earned $27.75 babysitting. She wants to buy jeans that cost $33.98. How much more money does she need to buy the jeans?

....

MULTIPLICATION WITH DECIMALS

Janice decided to buy an orange at the market and found that it cost $.80. When she found out that the price of the orange was so reasonable, she bought 5 more. How much did she spend on all of the oranges?

....

SUBTRACTION OF DECIMALS

Karen earned $27.75 babysitting. She wants to buy jeans that cost $33.98. How much more money does she need to buy the jeans?

Karen's money
needed
for jeans

$27.75 babysitting money	?

$33.98

$33.98 – $27.75 = $6.23

Karen needs $6.23 more to buy the jeans.

MULTIPLICATION WITH DECIMALS

Janice decided to buy an orange at the market and found that it cost $.80. When she found out that the price of the orange was so reasonable, she bought 5 more. How much did she spend on all of the oranges?

Janice's
oranges

.80	.80	.80	.80	.80	.80	?

6 X $.80 = $4.80

Janice spent $4.80 on all of the oranges.

MULTIPLICATION WITH DECIMALS

At a fishing derby on Saturday, George and Mario both caught fish. George's fish weighed 2.3 pounds. Mario's fish weighed twice as much as George's. What was the total weight of the 2 fish?

....

PERCENT

At graduation, 3/5 of the graduates received flowers. What percentage of graduates did *not* receive flowers at graduation?

....

MULTIPLICATION WITH DECIMALS

At a fishing derby on Saturday, George and Mario both caught fish. George's fish weighed 2.3 pounds. Mario's fish weighed twice as much as George's. What was the total weight of the 2 fish?

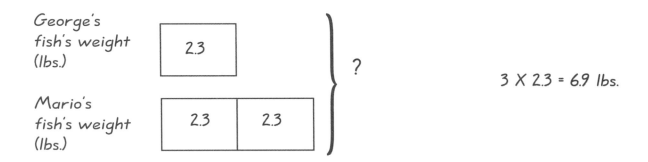

$3 \times 2.3 = 6.9$ lbs.

The total weight of the 2 fish was 6.9 pounds.

PERCENT

At graduation, 3/5 of the graduates received flowers. What percentage of graduates did *not* receive flowers at graduation?

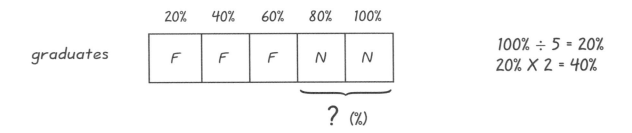

$100\% \div 5 = 20\%$
$20\% \times 2 = 40\%$

At graduation, 40% of the graduates did not receive flowers.

PERCENT

There were 250 people at an outdoor concert. Of these, 40% were children and the rest were adults. How many adults were at the concert?

PERCENT

Sabiana had $140. She spent 50% on clothes and 50% of the remaining money on books. She took the money she had left and put it in her savings account. How much money did Sabiana put in her savings account?

PERCENT

There were 250 people at an outdoor concert. Of these, 40% were children and the rest were adults. How many adults were at the concert?

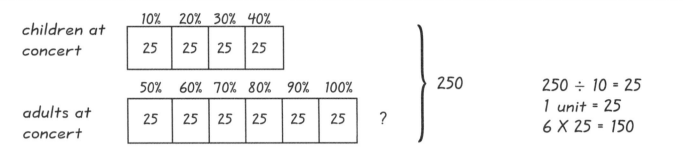

There were 150 adults at the outdoor concert.

PERCENT

Sabiana had $140. She spent 50% on clothes and 50% of the <u>remaining</u> money on books. She took the money she had left and put it in her savings account. How much money did Sabiana put in her savings account?

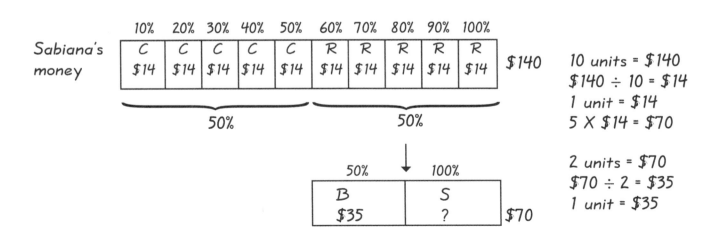

Sabiana put $35 in her savings account.

PERCENT

Of the 60 students in the third grade, we know that 60% are girls. We also know that 50% of the girls have blue eyes and 25% of the boys have blue eyes. How many of the students in the third grade have blue eyes?

MIXED OPERATIONS (+, – & ÷)

Frank and Rosa took a total of 7 minutes and 15 seconds to solve a math problem. If Rosa took 4 minutes and 5 seconds less than Frank, how long did Frank take to solve the problem?

PERCENT

Of the 60 students in the third grade, we know that 60% are girls. We also know that 50% of the girls have blue eyes and 25% of the boys have blue eyes. How many of the students in the third grade have blue eyes?

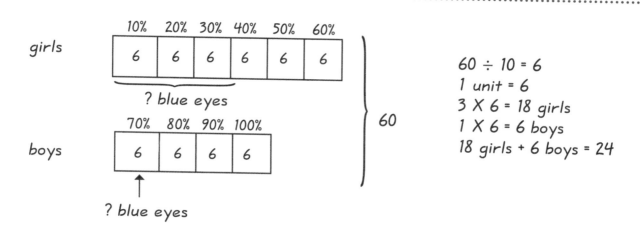

girls

10%	20%	30%	40%	50%	60%
6	6	6	6	6	6

? blue eyes

boys

70%	80%	90%	100%
6	6	6	6

↑
? blue eyes

} 60

60 ÷ 10 = 6
1 unit = 6
3 X 6 = 18 girls
1 X 6 = 6 boys
18 girls + 6 boys = 24

There are 24 students in the third grade who have blue eyes.

MIXED OPERATIONS (+, – & ÷)

Frank and Rosa took a total of 7 minutes and 15 seconds to solve a math problem. If Rosa took 4 minutes and 5 seconds less than Frank, how long did Frank take to solve the problem?

Frank's time to solve the math problem

| 1 min. 35 sec. | 4 min. 5 sec. | ? |

Rosa's time to solve the math problem

| 1 min. 35 sec. |

} 7 min. 15 sec.

7 min. 15 sec. – 4 min. 5 sec.
= 3 min. 10 sec.

3 min. 10 sec. ÷ 2
= 1 min. 35 sec.

1 min. 35 sec. + 4 min. 5 sec.
= 5 min. 40 sec.

Frank took 5 minutes and 40 seconds to solve the math problem.

ALGEBRA

Sara bought 26 treats for her 2 cats, Nick and Nack. She gave Nick 4 more treats than Nack. How many treats did each cat receive?

....

ALGEBRA

We know that 3/4 of a sum of money is $72. What is the sum of money?

....

ALGEBRA

Sara bought 26 treats for her 2 cats, Nick and Nack. She gave Nick 4 more treats than Nack. How many treats did each cat receive?

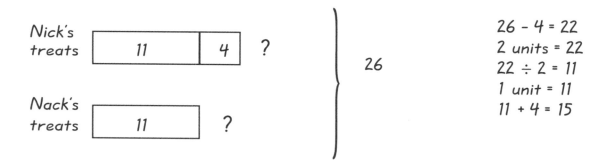

Nick's treats | 11 | 4 | ?

Nack's treats | 11 | ?

26

26 - 4 = 22
2 units = 22
22 ÷ 2 = 11
1 unit = 11
11 + 4 = 15

Nick received 15 treats and Nack received 11.

ALGEBRA

We know that 3/4 of a sum of money is $72. What is the sum of money?

money | $24 | $24 | $24 | $24 | ?

$72

3 units = $72
$72 ÷ 3 = $24
1 unit = $24
4 X $24 = $96

The sum of money is $96.

RESOURCES

PRINT & CD-ROM REFERENCES

American Institutes for Research (Alan Ginsburg, Steven Leinwand, Terry Anstrom, and Elizabeth Pollock). *What the United States Can Learn from Singapore's World-Class Mathematics System (and What Singapore Can Learn from the United States): An Exploratory Study*. Washington, DC: U.S. Department of Education Policy and Program Studies, January 28, 2005. Also available online at http://www.air.org/news/documents/singapore.htm.

Forsten, Char. *Math Strategies You Can Count On*. Peterborough, NH: Crystal Springs Books, 2005.

Forsten, Char. *Teaching Thinking and Problem Solving in Math*. New York: Scholastic Professional Books, 1992.

Hoerst, Jennifer. *Singapore Primary Mathematics Home Instructor's Guides: 2A and 2B*. (Guides are also available for grades 3–6.) Littleton, CO: Sonlight Curriculum Ltd., 2002.

Hof, David. "US, Singapore Agree to Cooperate on Math and Science." *Education Week*, September 18, 2002.

Hogan, Bob. *Singapore Math: Problem-Solving Secrets from the World's Math Leader*. CD-ROM. Peterborough, NH: Crystal Springs Books, 2005.

Ho Kheong, Dr. Fong. *The Essential Parents' Guide to Primary Maths*. Singapore: Marshall Cavendish, 2002.

Gowen, Annie. "East Meets West in Math Classes." *Washington Post*, October 21, 2000.

Kurtz, Michele. "State Tries New Techniques to Improve Math Education." *Boston Globe*, December 8, 2002.

Lee, Joseph D. *Primary Mathematics: Challenging Word Problems*, U.S. Edition (Grades 1–6). Singapore: SNP Panpac, 2004.

Ma, Liping. *Knowing and Teaching Elementary Mathematics*. Mahwah, NJ: Lawrence Erlbaum Associates, Inc., 1999.

National Center for Education Statistics, U.S. Department of Education. *The Third International Mathematics and Science Study (TIMSS)*. Washington, DC: U.S. Government Printing Office, 1995. Also available online at http://nces.ed.gov/timss//.

-----. *The Third International Mathematics and Science Study Repeat (TIMSS-R)*—Washington, DC: U.S. Government Printing Office, 1999. Also available online at http://nces.ed.gov/timss//.

-----. *The Trends in International Mathematics and Science Study (TIMSS)*. Formerly known as *The Third International Mathematics and Science Study*. Washington, DC: U.S. Government Printing Office, 2003. Also available online at http://nces.ed.gov/timss//.

Ng Chye Huat, Juliana (Mrs.) & Mrs. Lim Kian Huat. *A Handbook for Mathematics Teachers in Primary Schools*. Singapore: Federal Publications, 2001.

Parker, Thomas H., and Scott J. Baldridge. *Elementary Mathematics for Teachers*. Okemos, MI: Sefton-Ash Publishers, 2003.

Polya, George. *How to Solve It*. Princeton, NJ: Princeton University Press, 1945.

Quek, Tracy. "Now, Israel Uses S'pore Math Textbooks Too." *The Straits Times*, September 23, 2002.

Singapore Ministry of Education. *Primary Mathematics Textbooks, U.S. Editions: 1A, 1B, 2A, 2B, 3A, 3B, 4A, 4B, 5A, 5B, 6A,* and *6B.* Singapore: Marshall Cavendish, 2003.

Singapore Ministry of Education. "Singapore Number One in Mathematics Again and Rose to Number Two in Science in The Third International Mathematics and Science Study (TIMSS) 1999." November 28, 2000. Also available online at http://www.moe.gov.sg/press/2000/pr06122000.htm.

Singapore Primary Mathematics Teacher's Guides 1A and *1B*. Chicago: Rosenbaum Foundation, 2001.

Singapore Primary Mathematics Teacher's Guides, U.S. Editions: 2A, 2B, 3A, 3B, 4A, 4B, 5A, 5B, 6A, and 6B. Oregon City, OR: SingaporeMath.com Inc.

Strauss, Valerie. "Looking East for Math Techniques." *Washington Post*, March 21, 2000.

WEB SITES

Crystal Springs Books: www.crystalsprings.com

Bob Hogan's place value strips, disks, and cubes; *Primary Math* textbooks, workbooks, and teacher guides

SingaporeMath.com Inc.: www.singaporemath.com

Primary Math textbooks, workbooks, and teacher guides; Singapore Math information, curriculum descriptions, Web links, and other resources

Staff Development for Educators: www.sde.com

Training in Singapore Math

GRID FOR MODEL DRAWING

INDEX

Note: Page numbers in *italics* refer to "Hold These Thoughts" boxes.

Note: Page numbers in *italics* refer to "Hold These Thoughts" boxes.

Note: Page numbers in *italics* refer to "Hold These Thoughts" boxes.

Note: Page numbers in *italics* refer to "Hold These Thoughts" boxes.